INTERNAL AUDIT PRACTICES OF A CONSTRUCTION COMPANY IN SHANGHAI, CHINA: BASIS FOR AN ACTION PLAN

INTERNAL AUDIT PRACTICES OF A CONSTRUCTION COMPANY IN SHANGHAI, CHINA: BASIS FOR AN ACTION PLAN

Hu Mingyu

GALDA VERLAG 2025

Bibliografische Information der Deutschen Nationalbibliothek
Die Deutsche Nationalbibliothek verzeichnet diese Publikation in der Deutschen Nationalbibliografie; detaillierte bibliografische Daten sind im Internet über https://dnb.de abrufbar.

Originally presented as the author's thesis (doctoral):

ISBN 978-3-96203-426-9 (Print)
ISBN 978-3-96203-427-6 (E-Book)

TABLE OF CONTENTS

CHAPTER 2:
THEORETICAL FRAMEWORK

CHAPTER 3:
RESULTS AND DISCUSSION

ABSTRACT

The intention of the study was to determine the extent of internal audit practices' implementation in a construction company. This study employed a descriptive research design in which the research aimed to describe the extent to which the internal audit practices were being implemented construction company in Shanghai, China, in terms of the following sections: audit professionalism; performance audit; operating environment; and leadership and communication. Moreover, regarding the following areas of applied knowledge: professionalism, performance, environment, leadership, and communication, the objective of the study was to ascertain the level of competency of internal auditors. A total of 319 respondents were asked to voluntarily participate in the research study from a construction company. According to the internal audit practices' findings, the most extensively employed sections were operating environment and audit professionalism. Although the results indicated reasonable implementation, there were still inadequacies in the leadership and communication, and performance audit. Moreover, the internal auditors' level of applied knowledge competency was satisfactory. It was discovered that internal auditors were capable enough regarding their overall audit performance. However, it was discovered that it was crucial for internal auditors to fully comprehend their environment and develop their leadership abilities. It is necessary to consider about how they may convey the outcomes of their audit in a manner that is respectful of professionalism. Furthermore, the study determined that there were significant differences in the assessments of the respondents in terms of the extent to which the internal audit practices were being implemented and the level of competency of the internal auditors when they were grouped according to their profiles. The findings of the study served as the basis to develop an action plan in order to meet the contemporary demand for internal auditing competencies in the new normal. As a result, this could lead to operational effectiveness and financial stability, as well as protecting the assets of the construction company.

Keywords: action plan for internal auditors, construction company, internal audit practices, internal auditors, internal auditors' competencies

CHAPTER 1

INTRODUCTION

The Problem and its Background

The COVID-19 pandemic forced the majority of businesses to immediately switch to remote operations and implement internal auditing remotely, which necessitated some new auditing practices. The concern is whether the members of the internal audit team are properly trained to use those tools and systems, even though technology advancements make the physical auditing process simpler (Francis, 2022).

According to Gartner (2022), based on a survey of 166 audit leaders, the top challenge for audit managers is attracting talent with nontraditional skills to audit. A study conducted by Muruganandham et al. (2021) found that internal audits focus too much on compliance and not enough on improvements, and that auditing could be improved by, for example, developing auditors' applied knowledge and audit planning. These findings have practical implications for auditors auditing various management system standards as input for improving internal audit management practice.

A study conducted in China by Li et al. (2020), one of the key factors impeding the development of internal audit in the country is the indifference of internal audit by some listed construction enterprises. Due to the information asymmetry between shareholders and management that results from the majority of shareholders not actively participating in the operation and direction of the business, management may easily infringe on shareholders' interests.

Internal audit management is essential to providing the "checks and balances" that ensure enterprises' governance, risk management, and compliance processes, and it plays a crucial role in keeping enterprises on the right track. Internal audits help construction enterprises stay ahead of emerging risks by confirming that internal controls are functioning as they should (Dzikrullah et al., 2020; Farnham, 2021; Institute of Internal Auditors, 2021; Scherer, 2020).

Moreover, the Institute of Internal Auditors (2021) claims that internal auditors can identify operational inefficiencies, wasteful spending, employee theft, fraud, and instances of noncompliance with laws or regulations, saving the construction enterprise substantial funds and preserving its reputation in the marketplace.

In many nations, the construction industry contributes significantly to the GDP, making it a significant component of the global economy. Construction projects range from residential and commercial buildings to infrastructure projects like highways, bridges, and tunnels. It is a complicated and diversified sector. A vital management control method that can assist a construction company in identifying and reducing risks as well as increasing the efficacy and efficiency of its operations is internal auditing. However, there are various concerns and challenges with the existing state of professional auditors and the level of internal audit management in construction companies. There are issues like flawed management procedures, unusual audit methods, and insufficient audit resources, and some construction organizations have comparatively poor internal audit practices. These issues may make it difficult for companies to identify and mitigate risks, which would negatively impact how they operate and are managed. Due to a lack of skilled auditors, construction companies may assign audits to non-specialists or external auditors, which could produce inaccurate or insufficient audit results. Professional auditors are required to guarantee the accuracy and thoroughness of audits because construction companies are involved in various professional domains and require a wide variety of knowledge and skills.

As a result, the level of internal audit practices and the current situation with regard to professional auditors are significant problems in the management of construction companies that need to be addressed. The effectiveness and efficiency of internal audits in construction companies can be improved, and more value can be produced for the sustainable development of businesses, by establishing sound internal audit practices, training professional auditors, and establishing a reasonable and effective information sharing mechanism.

In addition, the relevant national laws and regulations stipulate the audit requirements and standards of construction companies, which will affect the requirements and standards of internal audit practices and professional auditors of construction companies. It is necessary to retrain and expand the original basic capabilities to ensure the high level and comprehensive quality of audit engineers and adapt to the new market demand.

This study aims to ascertain the extent to which the internal audit practice is being implemented in a particular construction company in Shanghai, China, in terms of the following sections: audit professionalism, performance audit, operating environment, and leadership and communication.

With this, it will provide the construction company with a comprehensive view of the data gathered about how the business is run, highlighting its strengths and areas for improvement. With regard to the following areas of applied knowledge: professionalism, performance, environment, leadership, and communication, the objective of the study is to ascertain the level of competency of internal auditors in the areas of applied knowledge.

The findings of the study will be utilized to develop an action plan in order to meet the contemporary demand for internal auditing competencies in the new normal. As a result, this will lead to operational effectiveness and financial stability, as well as protecting the assets of the construction company.

Significance of the Study

The intention of the study is to determine the extent of internal audit practices' implementation in a construction company. The study's findings will be put to use in order to improve internal management audit procedures that result in operational effectiveness, financial stability, and asset protection for the construction enterprise.

Internal Auditors. The findings of the study will be most beneficial to the members of the internal auditors. This will serve as a basis for formulating professional development among the members of the audit committees in order to improve the current internal audit practices of the construction company. The findings will serve as a cornerstone to identify gaps in the areas of internal audit applied knowledge competencies that must be acquired by the internal auditors and uplift their auditing capabilities.

Managers. The insights that will be found, the identified gaps, and the outcomes of the investigations will be significant factors in determining how the construction enterprise managers will be able to improve their current internal audit practices and assess what particular actions should be taken to address the gaps in the current level of competencies of their internal auditors.

Construction Company. The results of the study, in terms of the challenge in the extent of implementation and the applied knowledge gaps in the internal auditors' current level of competencies, will act as a foundation for improving management audit practices and guarantee efficient company governance, risk management, and compliance systems that add value and enhance the company's operations.

Researcher. The findings of this study will assist the researcher in understanding the significance of an effective implementation of internal audit practices to identify operational inefficiencies, fraud, and instances of noncompliance with standards, saving the construction company substantial funds and preserving its reputation in the business world. The findings will also serve as a basis for the researcher to recommend an action plan for the internal auditors to uplift their skills in terms of the areas of applied knowledge of internal audit competencies.

Future Researchers. The study's findings will serve as a foundation and set of internal audit practices guidelines for future research or studies of a similar nature for more generalization of the findings or outputs. Moreover, the end result of the study will provide future researchers with a greater overview of how the level of applied knowledge competencies of the internal auditors affect the extent of implementation of internal management audit practice of a construction enterprise.

Review of Related Literature

This presents the review of the relevant literature and studies. The following variables were found to be significant in the conceptualization of the study.

Internal Audit

A company's ability to accomplish its goals and protect its assets is significantly aided by internal audit practice (Alqudah et al. 2019). Additionally, internal audit has evolved into a crucial management tool for enterprises looking to implement effective control (Behrend & Eulerich 2019; Endaya & Hanefah 2016). Having a strong internal audit practice is crucial for construction enterprises; the role, as defined by The International Professional Practices Framework for Internal Auditing (IPPF), has a significant impact on enhancing the efficiency of an enterprise's risk management, internal control, and governance processes (The Institute of Internal Auditors 2017). Internal auditing is described as "an independent, objective assurance and consulting activity designed to add value and improve an organization's operations" by The Institute of Internal Auditors. By bringing a systematic, disciplined approach to evaluate and enhance the effectiveness of risk management, control, and governance processes, it aids a company in achieving its goals (The Institute of Internal Auditors 2017). Additionally, the audit committee, senior management, and external auditor of an enterprise value efficient internal audit.

Likewise, an unbiased evaluation of the operations, procedures, and performance of the entire enterprise is provided to the audit committee and senior management by the internal audit (The Institute of Internal Auditors 2017). Senior management relies on internal audit to strengthen controls, lower risk, and improve operations, while the audit committee relies on internal audit to establish strong internal controls, produce high-quality financial reporting, and maintain regulatory compliance (Eulerich et al. 2019).

Internal Audit Practices

In accordance with the Institute of Internal Auditors (2022), internal audit is an objective, balanced guarantee and consulting activity whose goal is to benefit the company and enhance operational effectiveness. To evaluate risk management, control, and governance procedures, as well as to increase their effectiveness in support of enterprise objectives, requires a systematic and standardized approach. It is clear from this that the Institute of Internal Auditors places great emphasis on the legitimacy and objectivity of financial audits and provides detailed instructions on the techniques and procedures for conducting fraud audits.

The objective of an internal audit is to safeguard the interests of the company's shareholders generally, but management may resent internal audit work to some extent because they are pursuing their own interests (Li et al., 2020). Li et al. (2020) claim that there are two main ways in which this negative behavior shows up. One is that internal audit problems are not addressed by management, and the other is that internal auditors' logical recommendations are not taken into account. The internal auditor in China is losing confidence in their own work and sense of accountability as a result of the current situation, which also makes it difficult for the internal audit work to proceed normally. As a result, listed companies' internal audit efforts have not been as effective as they should have been.

Additionally, listed companies play a significant role in China's economic growth. It is urgently necessary to establish a set of systems suitable for their own evaluation, supervision, and risk management in order to enhance corporate governance due to the diversification of their operating procedures and the complexity of their property rights structures. Internal audit is a crucial component of corporate governance and plays a significant role. There are numerous flaws in the development process as a result of China's internal audit's tardy beginning and its rapid development (Li et al. 2020).

According to Scherer (2020), the internal audit function operates from within, acting as watchdogs over the enterprise's accountability and integrity, scrutinizing the financial reporting, preventing fraud, mistakes, and risks, and offering unbiased assurance that the entity is adhering to the rules and standards that it should. Additionally, internal audits can assist the construction company in preventing financial loss.

The are six benefits of internal auditing as claimed by Scherer (2020):

Reliable Internal Controls. The first task for the internal auditor should be to assess the control environment for the company. The internal controls, which include actions, systems, and processes—including monitoring—are evaluated by internal audits to make sure they are well-designed, implemented, and operating as they should—regardless of who fills which role. Internal control is a procedure carried out by a company's management, board of directors, and other employees and is intended to give reasonable assurance about the accomplishment of goals related to compliance, reporting, and operations.

Efficiency. Internal audits identify overlaps in your governance processes, company practices, and operational procedures. They then make recommendations for how to streamline these areas to save time and money.

Security. Internal audits examine the cybersecurity environment, counting all of the digital devices and checking to see if they are secured in accordance with the policies, among other things. Additionally, they scan the digital systems and networks for weaknesses and offer suggestions on how to plug holes.

Integrity. Internal audits examine and scrutinize the financial statements to ensure their accuracy and integrity because individuals are not always truthful.

Reduced Risk. Internal audits examine whether the risk mitigations are operating as intended and take into account all the risks to the construction company that have been identified. Where they are not, audit reports will outline what the construction company should do to fix the problem.

Improved Compliance. Internal audits examine whether the construction enterprise is actually in compliance with the laws, regulations, and industry standards with which it must comply. Where the construction company falls short, auditors offer suggestions for how to fix the issue.

Audit Professionalism

In an internal audit, professional judgment refers to the use of relevant knowledge and experience within the parameters set by auditing standards and professional behavior regulations to make an appropriate decision when there are several possible courses of action. There is no set method for using professional judgment, but good use of professional judgment is seen as a crucial component of an internal auditor's performance, and improving judgment skills is crucial for auditors (Heyrani et al., 2016).

The likelihood of enterprise fraud is rising along with the intensity of global competition. Due to the current circumstances, it is very likely that numerous violations and irregularities will have serious repercussions that could hurt numerous parties, such as the occurrence of fraud. Fraud is an action that happens when there is a chance to make false statements in financial reports and false statements resulting from the improper handling of assets (Tuanakotta, 2016).

The attempt to conceal, falsify, mislead, manipulate, and alter the right and fair view in order to obtain illicit gain at the expense of another person is a common aspect of fraud, which is a serious problem (Abdullahi & Mansor, 2015). Professionalism has become the primary requirement for auditors in carrying out their responsibilities in order to maintain public confidence in the caliber of investigation and fraud prevention. An auditor will be more professional if their professional dimension level is higher (Dwi & Effendi, 2016).

With the above situations, the professionalism of internal auditors, according to Paranoan (2018), is the key to running a successful business. Professional internal auditors will perform their duties well, including helping management prevent and identify fraud that happens in the workplace. However, the internal auditors' professional demeanor is insufficient if they lack a culture of honesty, high ethics, and management accountability to assess the risks and other circumstances that might exist on the part of the offender.

Performance Audit

According to The Institute of Internal Auditors (2021), monitoring the effectiveness of the internal audit activity has many advantages, including:

- Improving comprehension of internal audit's efficacy and productivity.
- Having confidence that internal auditing efforts support the corporate, board, and management committee's strategic goals.
- Getting insightful updates on important issues, such as the efficiency of controls and risk management.
- Finding information about chances to increase the effectiveness and/or efficiency of the internal audit activity.
- Being aware of how to improve interactions with external auditors and other third parties as necessary.
- Providing more opportunities for open communication, including direct feedback from internal audit and helpful criticism from the board or management committee, which can enhance engagement quality and solidify the bond between the management committee and internal audit.

Every company has a purpose, according to Praise and Rapina (2022). However, in order to accomplish these objectives, the enterprise faces risk-related uncertainty constraints that may prevent it from achieving its objectives. In order to achieve enterprise goals as effectively as possible, effective risk management is required to reduce the risks that may arise. Many construction companies still struggle to manage risks effectively and may not even fully comprehend the purpose of risk management. As a result, they are forced to deal with risks that could jeopardize their ability to achieve enterprise objectives, risks that could be reduced or even completely avoided.

Furthermore, the role of internal auditing is rarely involved in developing and implementing strategies. In a rapidly evolving business environment where construction companies face more risks than ever, stakeholders should be more knowledgeable about new risks and how to manage them in order to safeguard the company from setbacks that could obstruct its strategic goals (Nabulsi & Haidoura, 2018).

Operating Environment

Internal auditors' responsibilities have changed from determining the risks associated with financial statement audits to ensuring the environmental management system's legitimacy. The discussion of internal auditors has expanded to include consultancy, supervision, prevention, protection, and evaluation. A new interpretation of the roles of internal auditors has also emerged (Chambers & Odar, 2015). Internal control generally aims to ensure that the enterprise is run effectively and economically.

The ability of the company to withstand pressure from both internal and external sources is impacted by establishing a strong control environment through the display of integrity and ethical values, appropriate monitoring processes, the existence of adequate duty segregation, and a sense of responsibility for achieving goals. Companies with more effective internal audits typically have a more developed control environment (supporting control environment) in terms of awareness of the value of risk and control compared to those with less effective internal audits (Barii & Tuek, 2016).

Furthermore, a study by Sukirman et al. (2021) demonstrated that internal auditors have a significant impact on operating environments in the same way that environmental control has an impact on good governance. As a result, the internal auditor plays a helpful role in putting good governance into practice. Thus, all kinds of companies can greatly benefit from good governance. In order to improve the efficiency of environmental control and internal auditors and achieve good governance, management must cooperate reasonably.

Leadership

A recent study of over 1,600 chief audit executives, senior management, and board members was published by professional services specialists, and it found that internal audit functions with very effective leadership function better and add more value to their companies (Olavsrud, 2016).

According to Olavsrud (2016), the top internal audit leaders share five characteristics that all chief audit executives should emulate. These characteristics are as follows:

Create and Follow Through on A Vision. It was discovered that highly effective internal audit leaders have a clear vision that is in line with the expectations of stakeholders as well as the strategic direction of their company. These leaders transform their visions into strategic plans and invest in the capabilities needed to realize them, particularly in data analytics and other modern tools that let them make process innovations.

Source and Retain the Right Talent. The biggest obstacle to them increasing their leadership contributions has been identified as a lack of talent. Additional new skills are required as business transformation continues to develop. Two talent behaviors distinguish the most effective internal audit leaders from the competition: a focus on mentoring and talent development and the capacity to find the right talent when required.

Empower the Internal Audit Function. The authority within the organization and the cooperation of stakeholders are crucial factors in the efficiency of internal audit leaders. It was discovered that vice presidents or other senior positions are held by 78% of very effective internal audit leaders. Furthermore, it was discovered that stakeholders are drawn to more experienced leadership candidates to fill the position of internal audit leaders, noting that it is their duty to empower them by fostering a culture that recognizes the value of a robust control environment.

Demonstrate Executive Presence. It was discovered that 90% of very effective internal audit leaders excel in exhibiting executive presence, underscoring the necessity for leadership talent in the internal auditor's role. They offer audacious viewpoints and have big ideas for the business. It states that internal audit leaders must gain the trust of stakeholders by informing, educating, and influencing them. Communication with a variety of internal and external stakeholders, each of whom has a different expectation of the function, is one of the trickier challenges internal audit leaders must overcome.

Establishing Strong Trust. The most successful internal audit leaders distinguish themselves by forging significant relationships with the business. To become a very effective frontrunner, internal audit leaders should be able to demonstrate three distinct behaviors: (1) build relationships based on trust; (2) collaborate with other assurance functions to play greater roles in coordinating risk management across functions; and (3) use those connections to increase their level of engagement throughout the organization by taking on leadership roles in working with management, compliance, and legal departments.

Communication

According to Whitehouse (2016), internal audit leaders need to develop a variety of skills that are not always emphasized as being a part of the audit profession in order to provide the most value to their audit committees. However, auditors cannot be truly great without excellent communication and presentation skills to present their findings.

The success of internal audits in an organization also depends on efficient and effective communication. Nevertheless, it is asserted that a significant issue for internal auditing in many enterprises is a lack of effective communication. A lifeline connecting management and auditors in an organization is effective communication (Gurama, 2019).

According to Gurama (2019), internal auditors must maintain excellent communication skills in order to advance and succeed in an organization's complex, dynamic, and diverse auditing environment. As a result, an internal auditor needs to improve their interpersonal, listening, written, and oral communication skills to facilitate their performance and effectively carry out their duties.

Low Quality of Internal Auditors

As claimed by Li et al. (2020), Chinese listed companies' internal auditors' poor performance is primarily seen in two areas.

On the one hand, listed company internal auditors only practice one profession, and as a result, the overall quality falls short of what is required for registered company internal audits. Internal auditors in China tend to have backgrounds in either accounting or auditing. Internal auditors with additional professional backgrounds in information technology are less common. The single professional composition of internal auditors cannot meet the needs of internal audit in the background of information technology, resulting in low internal audit efficiency from the perspective of the audit scope covered by the internal audit of listed enterprises (Li et al., 2020).

On the other hand, the total number of talents in the auditing industry in China is growing as a result of years of development, but the majority of senior auditing talents primarily work for social audit institutions like accounting firms. Internal auditors with strong theoretical backgrounds are scarce in the listed enterprise's internal audit department (Li et al., 2020).

Internal Auditors' Competencies

According to The Institute of Internal Auditors (2022), internal auditors need to possess a wide range of applied knowledge competencies.

These competencies include professionalism, performance, environment, leadership, and communications.

Professionalism. Competencies necessary to show the authority, credibility, and moral behavior necessary for a successful internal audit activity.

Performance. Competencies necessary to plan and carry out internal audit engagements in accordance with the standards.

Environment. Competencies needed to recognize and manage risks particular to the organization's industry and environment.

Leadership and Communication. Competencies needed to manage internal audit staff and procedures as well as communicate effectively, build relationships, and provide strategic direction.

According to Competency-Based Framework for Internal Auditors (2021) in Bhutan, The gaps between desired capability and current capability are the areas where training is required. The process of identifying the skills gap and training requirements for internal auditors is called an analysis of their training needs. The process is used to ascertain whether the training will produce a solution to the issue. It makes sure that training is directed at the right employees, the right competencies, and the right departmental needs. By giving the internal auditors the necessary knowledge that can be applied significantly, the training can narrow, if not completely close, the gap. Building and enhancing an employee's capability and competency should be a shared responsibility between the department and the employee.

Likewise, it is imperative for internal auditors to develop specific applied knowledge competencies to perform the required tasks efficiently. Creating an individual development plan based on improved internal management audit practice would allow individuals to assess whether they meet the competencies required of their applied knowledge level and work on performance gaps (Competency-Based Framework for Internal Auditors, 2021).

The Internal Audit Practices in China

Internal audit practices in China have undergone significant changes in recent years, driven by increased regulatory scrutiny and the need for organizations to improve their risk management practices. This literature review provides an overview of key research on internal audit management in China, highlighting trends, challenges, and best practices.

One key trend in China's internal audit management is the growing importance of risk management. A study by Li and Li (2018) found that Chinese companies are increasingly focused on identifying and mitigating risk, and that the internal audit function plays a critical role in this process. The authors recommend that internal auditors in China adopt a more proactive approach to risk management, rather than simply focusing on compliance.

Another important trend is the increasing use of technology in internal audit management. A study by He and Chen (2019) found that Chinese companies are investing in technology to improve their internal audit processes, including the use of data analytics, artificial intelligence, and blockchain. The authors suggest that these technologies can help internal auditors in China identify risks more quickly and accurately, and improve the efficiency and effectiveness of their audits.

Chinese companies are struggling to attract and retain high-quality internal auditors, which can hinder their ability to effectively manage risk and comply with regulations.

Another challenge is the complex regulatory environment in China. A study by Wu et al. (2019) found that Chinese companies face a wide range of regulatory requirements related to internal audit management, including requirements for independence, competence, and objectivity. The authors suggest that companies in China should invest in developing internal audit policies and procedures that comply with local regulations, and that they should work closely with regulators to stay up-to-date with any changes.

In terms of best practices, there is growing recognition of the need for internal auditors in China to adopt a more strategic approach to risk management. A study by Liu et al. (2018) recommends that Chinese companies should focus on integrating their internal audit function with their overall risk management strategy, and prioritize areas of high risk and potential impact.

Another best practice that has emerged in China's internal audit management is the importance of building a culture of compliance and ethics. A study by Chen and Li (2019) found that Chinese companies that have a strong ethical culture are more likely to have effective internal audit processes and to comply with regulations. The authors suggest that companies in China should prioritize building a culture of compliance through training and communication programs, and by rewarding ethical behavior.

The important area of focus is stakeholder engagement. A study by Wang et al. (2020) found that internal auditors in China should engage more closely with key stakeholders, including senior management, the board of directors, and external auditors. The authors recommend that internal auditors should communicate their findings and recommendations more effectively, and should work collaboratively with other stakeholders to improve risk management and compliance. There is growing recognition of the importance of international standards and best practices in internal audit management. A study by Zhang and Zhang (2019) found that Chinese companies are increasingly adopting international standards, such as the International Professional Practices Framework (IPPF), to guide their internal audit processes. The authors suggest that Chinese companies should continue to learn from global best practices and benchmark their internal audit processes against international standards.

China's internal audit management landscape is complex and evolving rapidly, with a range of trends, challenges, and best practices. To be successful, internal auditors in China should focus on building a culture of compliance and ethics, leveraging technology, engaging stakeholders, and adopting international standards and best practices. By doing so, they can help their organizations effectively manage risk, comply with regulations, and achieve their strategic objectives.

Another key aspect of internal audit management in China is the role of the government and regulatory bodies. The National Audit Office of China (CNAO) is the main regulatory body overseeing all internal audit activities in China, including those conducted by government agencies and state-owned enterprises. A study by Wang and Sun (2021) found that the Chinese government has been increasingly focused on strengthening internal audit regulation and promoting the development of the internal audit profession.

The study also identified several challenges facing internal audit management in China, including a lack of professional standards and guidelines, as well as limited resources and training opportunities for internal auditors. The authors suggest that the government could play a more active role in promoting the development of the internal audit profession by providing more resources and support, and by encouraging the adoption of international standards and best practices.

The key issue is the need for internal auditors in China to balance their roles as both auditors and advisors. A study by Li and Li (2020) found that internal auditors in China are increasingly being asked to provide advisory services to their organizations, in addition to traditional audit functions. The authors suggest that internal auditors should adopt a more balanced approach, focusing on both auditing and advising, and that they should work closely with management to ensure that their advice is aligned with the organization's strategic goals.

The Growing Recognition of the Importance of Internal Audit Quality in China

A study by Liu et al. (2021) found that companies in China with high-quality internal audit processes are more likely to achieve better financial performance and have higher levels of corporate social responsibility. The authors suggest that companies in China should prioritize investing in their internal audit function, including hiring and retaining skilled auditors, adopting advanced technologies, and promoting a culture of continuous improvement.

In conclusion, internal audit management in China is a dynamic and complex field with a range of trends, challenges, and best practices. To be successful, internal auditors in China should balance their roles as auditors and advisors, leverage technology, and focus on building a culture of continuous improvement and quality. Additionally, the government and regulatory bodies should continue to promote the development of the internal audit profession and encourage the adoption of international standards and best practices.

Challenges of Internal Audit Practices in China's Construction Industry

Internal audit management plays a crucial role in ensuring the effectiveness and efficiency of operations, compliance with regulations and standards, and risk management in the construction industry. In China, the construction industry is facing various challenges related to the internal audit management system.

One of the main challenges is the lack of qualified internal auditors. The majority of internal auditors in China's construction industry lack professional qualifications and experience, which affects the quality and effectiveness of internal audits (Zhang & Xu, 2019). Another challenge is the limited independence of internal auditors, as they may be influenced by external factors, such as management or political pressures(Zhao & Li, 2019).

Furthermore, there are concerns regarding the quality of internal audit reports, which may not reflect the true status of the company's operations, risks, and internal control systems(Zhou, 2020). In addition, there is a lack of integration between the internal audit management system and other management systems, such as risk management, quality management, and environmental management, which leads to inefficiencies and duplication of efforts (Cao & Zhang, 2020).

To address these challenges, the Chinese government has implemented various measures to improve internal audit management in the construction industry. For example, the government has strengthened the training and certification of internal auditors, introduced regulations to enhance the independence of internal auditors, and encouraged the integration of internal audit management with other management systems (Wang & Wu, 2020).

In addition to the challenges mentioned in the previous response, another significant challenge for internal audit management in China's construction industry is the lack of standardization and consistency in internal audit practices. The lack of clear standards and guidelines for internal audit management makes it difficult for construction companies to conduct effective internal audits and assess their own internal audit functions (Li et al., 2021).

Moreover, there is also a lack of communication and coordination between internal auditors and other departments within construction companies. This can lead to a lack of understanding and support for internal audit functions, as well as duplication of efforts and inefficient use of resources (Zhao & Li, 2019). The COVID-19 pandemic has also posed new challenges for internal audit management in China's construction industry. With the rapid shift to remote work and virtual collaboration, internal audit teams have had to adapt to new technologies and communication methods to conduct audits and communicate with other departments (Cao & Zhang, 2020). The COVID-19 pandemic has had a significant impact on internal audit management in various industries, including the construction industry in China. With the implementation of lockdown, social distancing measures, and remote work policies, internal audit teams have had to adapt their management practices to ensure business continuity and effective risk management.

One of the key challenges for internal audit management during the COVID-19 pandemic is the need for remote audits. With many employees working remotely, it may be difficult to access the necessary data and systems for conducting audits. As a result, internal audit teams have had to rely on technology such as video conferencing and remote access tools to conduct audits (Deloitte, 2021). Another challenge is the increased risk of fraud and cyber attacks during the pandemic. With the disruption to business operations and the increase in remote work, there is a greater risk of fraud and cyber attacks. Internal audit teams have had to be vigilant in identifying and mitigating these risks (PwC, 2021).

In addition, the pandemic has highlighted the importance of risk management and business continuity planning. Internal audit teams have had to work closely with management to identify and assess risks related to the pandemic and develop plans to mitigate these risks (KPMG, 2021). Overall, the COVID-19 pandemic has brought about significant changes to internal audit management in the construction industry in China, with the increased use of technology, a focus on risk management and business continuity planning, and the need for greater flexibility and adaptability in management practices.

To address these challenges, there is a need for greater collaboration and communication between internal auditors and other departments within construction companies, as well as the development of standardized guidelines and best practices for internal audit management (Li et al., 2021). The use of new technologies and digital tools may also help to improve the efficiency and effectiveness of internal audit management in the construction industry (Cao & Zhang, 2020).

Improved Internal Audit Practices

The objective of having the internal management audit of a construction company is not only to complete general internal audit tasks, but also to provide useful internal audit information for effective resource evaluation, in order to maximize the use of the company's resources. The aim of setting up an institutional assessment system includes higher expectations for internal management audit findings (Li et al., 2020).

The improved management internal audit should be factual, precise, timely, appropriate, valid, and realistic. It should report not only the true state of the construction enterprise's internal audit, but also the state of internal control. The improved internal management audit practice should report not only internal audit data, but also related risk prediction information; not only internal financial audit information, but also related internal control information; not only monetary information, but also non-monetary relevant data. In an essence, improved internal management audit practice is the "work product" of improved internal audit work (Li et al., 2020).

CHAPTER 2

THEORETICAL FRAMEWORK

The study is anchored to the Agency Theory by Kathleen M. Eisenhardt in 1989.

Figure 1

Diagram of Agent Theory

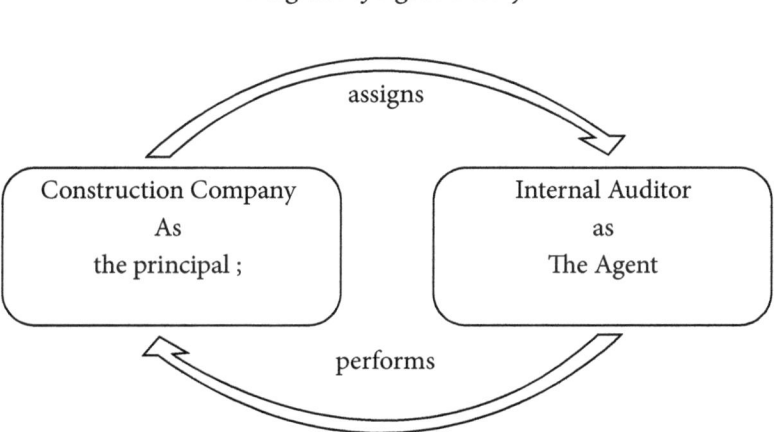

Agency Theory

A contract between a construction company as the principal and its internal auditors as an agent, which could be referred to as an agency relationship. Internal auditors collaborate with the construction company as agents to carry out some tasks on the board of directors' behalf. The board also grants internal auditors some decision-making authority because managers might abuse their powers in order to further their own interests. As a result, the presence of internal auditors and their team members will aid the construction company in improving performance while also ensuring that management executes its plans in line with standards.

According to Endaya and Hanefah (2019), the board and management are just two examples of the various internal audit users who internal auditors act as agents and monitors for. When the board is dysfunctional and management is likely to exert significant control over the internal audit, agency issues may arise. If this intricate concern proves to be ineffective, it poses a problem for internal auditors who must carry out their operational monitoring duties. Internal auditors are frequently employed by management, but they also serve as the board of directors' delegates because the board has confidence in their capacity to assess management's performance.

Internal auditors, acting as agents, are required to conduct internal audits at a professional level, necessitating applied knowledge competencies in areas such as professionalism, performance, environment, leadership, and communication. The board's confidence in the internal auditor's competence would increase if internal auditors met these requirements and there were training programs in place. Internal auditors can also disprove accusations of neglecting their duties by demonstrating that they were performed in accordance with their professional level.

The chief audit executive, who is primarily in charge of developing the internal audit plan, reporting internal audit findings, and implementing internal audit recommendations, oversees the work of the internal auditors. The internal audit department is a resource that the members of internal audit rely on to fulfill their obligation to evaluate the internal control system. Internal auditors must gather enough trustworthy data during this evaluation to support their evaluation of the internal control system. The presence of such proof will boost the construction company's level of confidence in the internal auditors' work. Therefore, for construction companies to view internal auditors as agents, the effectiveness of the internal audit department is a crucial requirement.

As representatives of the construction company, internal auditors rely on their support. Internal auditors' independence is increased and management interference in internal audit's scope or performance is decreased when there is a strong committee in place in the construction industry.

Based on the discussion above, the agency theory is a valuable theory that can explain the relationship between certain study variables and that it is pertinent to be included in the development of this research's improved internal audit practices in the construction company.

Conceptual Framework

The conceptual framework of the study is anchored in Figure 2 below, which corresponds to the study's research paradigm.

The input of the study involves the following: the profile of the respondents that includes age, sex, educational attainment, and length of years at the company; the extent to which internal audit practices are being implemented by a construction company in Shanghai, China, in terms of the following sections: audit professionalism; performance audit; operating environment; and leadership and communication; and the level of applied knowledge competency of the internal auditors in terms of its following areas: professionalism, performance, environment, leadership, and communication.

The process of the study involves the collection of data through a self-made, validated research instrument. The data collected from the involved construction company will be tabulated.

Likewise, these will be subjected to statistical treatment using appropriate statistical tools to determine the significant difference in the respondents' assessments on the extent of implementation of internal audit practices and the level of applied knowledge competency of the internal auditors.

The outputs of the study will be used to develop an action plan to improve internal audit practices in order to meet modern demands for operational effectiveness and financial stability as well as to protect the assets of the construction company.

Figure 2

Research Paradigm of the Study

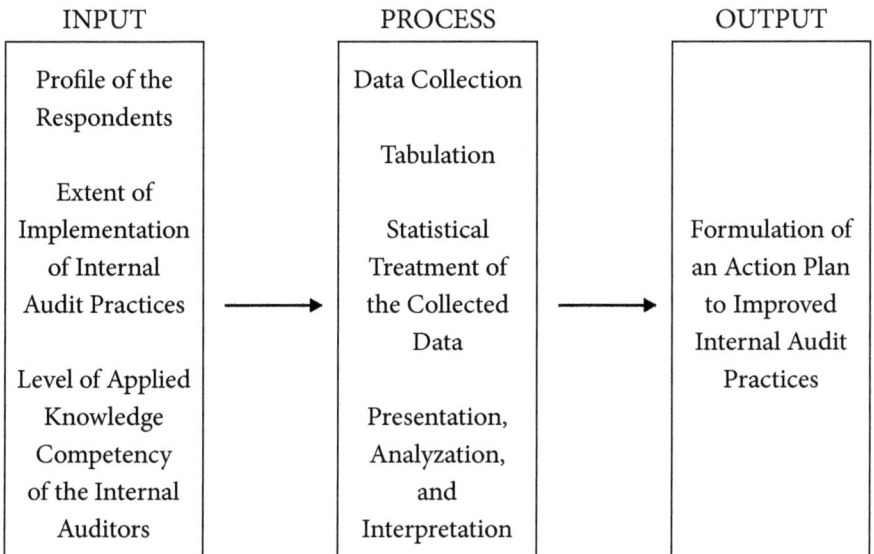

Statement of the Problem

The study's aim is to determine the extent to which internal audit practices are being implemented in a construction company. The study's findings will be used to formulate an action plan to improve internal audit practices, resulting in operational effectiveness, financial stability, and asset protection.

Before delving into the statement of the problem, it is essential to revisit the demographic profile of the respondents in relation to the extent of implementation of internal audit practices and the level of applied knowledge competency of the internal auditors. Examining the demographic characteristics of the respondents, such as age, gender, education, and experience, provides valuable insights into how these factors may impact the implementation of internal audit practices and the competency levels of the auditors. Understanding the relationship between demographics and the extent of implementation of internal audit practices will enable us to assess whether certain demographic groups exhibit variations in their adoption and utilization of these practices. Similarly, exploring the relationship between demographics and the level of applied knowledge competency will help identify any variations in the skill levels and expertise of internal auditors across different demographic groups. By comprehensively analyzing these relationships, the study aims to uncover potential factors that influence the successful implementation of internal audit practices and the development of applied knowledge competency among internal auditors, contributing to the overall understanding of the research problem.

Specifically, the study seeks out to answer the following questions:

1. What is the profile of the respondents in terms of the following:

    1.1 age;

    1.2 sex;

    1.3 educational attainment; and

    1.4 length of years at the company?

2. What is the extent to which the internal audit practices are being implemented by a construction company in Shanghai, China, in terms of the following sections:

    2.1 audit professionalism;

    2.2 performance audit;

2.3 operating environment; and

2.4 leadership and communication?

3. What is the level of applied knowledge competency of the internal auditors in a construction company in Shanghai, China, in terms of the following areas of applied knowledge:

3.1 professionalism;

3.2 performance;

3.3 environment;

3.4 leadership; and

3.5 communication?

4. Is there a significant difference in the assessments of the respondents in terms of the extent to which the internal audit practices are being implemented when grouped according to their profiles?

5. Is there a significant difference in the assessment of the respondents in terms of the level of competency of the internal auditors when grouped according to their profiles?

6. How may the result of the study be utilized to develop an action plan for the construction company to improve its internal audit practices?

Hypotheses of the Study

The research study will be established on the following hypotheses resulting from the problem:

1. There is no significant difference in the assessments of the respondents in terms of the extent to which the internal audit practices are being implemented when grouped according to their profile.

2. There is no significant difference in the assessment of the respondents in terms of the level of competency of the internal auditors when grouped according to their profile.

Definition of Terms

The following concepts used in this study are operationally defined for better understanding and clarity:

Audit Professionalism. This pertains to internal management audit practices that involve the mission of internal auditing, internal audit charter, enterprise independence, individual objectivity, ethical behavior, due professional care, and professional development.

Communication. This corresponds to an area of applied knowledge competencies needed by internal auditors to manage internal audit staff and processes as well as communicate effectively, maintain relationships, and manage relationships.

Environment. This pertains to an area where internal auditors' applied knowledge competencies are needed to recognize and address risks specific to the industry and environment in which the enterprise operates.

Internal Audit Practices. This refers to a management practices that is crucial for an internal audit system as it ensures that the enterprise's governance, risk management, and compliance processes are carried out in a way that will add value and enhance its operations.

Leadership and Communication. These are internal management audit practices of an enterprise that include strategic planning and management of internal audit, audit plans and coordination of assurance efforts, improvement programs, and communication like relationships, advocacy, and reports.

Leadership. This refers to an area where internal auditors must demonstrate applied knowledge competencies in order to provide strategic direction for the management of internal audit personnel and procedures.

Operating Environment. This refers to internal management audit practices of an enterprise that involves organizational strategic planning and management, business process, social responsibility and sustainability, and accounting and finance.

Performance Audit. This pertains to internal management audit practices of an enterprise that involves, governance, fraud, risk management, internal control, engagement planning, fieldwork, and outcomes.

Performance. This pertains to an area where internal auditors must possess applied knowledge competencies in order to plan and carry out internal audit engagements in conformance with the standards.

Professionalism. This is relevant to an area where internal auditors must demonstrate their applied knowledge competencies in order to establish the authority, credibility, and ethical behavior necessary for a successful internal audit activity.

Scope and Delimitation of the Study

The respondents of the study will include internal auditors and managers from a construction company in Shanghai, China.

The internal auditor respondents that will be involved in the study are appointed members of the board of directors of the construction company. They have knowledge of the internal audit system of the construction company and concrete experience with the extent to which the internal audit practices are being implemented. Also, they are aware of the level of their current competency in terms of applied knowledge in the areas of internal auditing.

The manager respondents that will be asked to participate in the study are managers, which includes members of the board, executives, department heads, and other similar positions with knowledge on how internal audit practices are being implemented and how members of the internal auditors have been conducting internal audits in their construction company. Their insights, observations, and assessments will be significant factors in determining how the construction company will be able to improve its current internal audit practices and assess what actions should be taken to address the current level of competencies of their internal auditors.

The study will be conducted at Greenland Real Estate Development Group, a research locale located in Shanghai, China.

The study will be limited to an assessment of the extent to which the internal audit practices are being implemented by a construction company in terms of the following sections: audit professionalism, performance audit, operating environment, and leadership and communication. Moreover, the level of applied knowledge competency of the internal auditors will be limited to its areas, namely: professionalism, performance, environment, leadership, and communication.

The study will not involve managers who do not have knowledge of the extent to which the internal audit practices are being implemented.

Research Design

This study will employ descriptive research design in which the research aims to describe the extent to which the internal audit practices are being implemented construction company in Shanghai, China, in terms of the following sections: audit professionalism; performance audit; operating environment; and leadership and communication.

Moreover, regarding the following areas of applied knowledge: professionalism, performance, environment, leadership, and communication, the objective of the study is to ascertain the level of competency of internal auditors.

According to McCombes (2022a), descriptive research design aims to describe a population, situation, or phenomenon accurately and systematically. It is a type of quantitative research that is an appropriate choice when the research aim is to identify and describe characteristics and phenomena.

Additionally, the study will also use survey as a type of descriptive research. This is a flexible method of data collection that can be used in many different types of research. Survey research means collecting information about a group of people by asking them questions and analyzing the results (McCombes, 2022b). In order to achieve content validity, this study was based on relevant theories, and the questionnaire design was carried out with reference to existing empirical research and revised. After the first draft of the questionnaire is completed, it will be discussed and revised according to the validity of experts' opinions and the evaluation of the interview. Therefore, the content validity of the variable can be guaranteed to a certain extent.

The analysis of the results will be utilized to develop an action plan to improve internal practices in order to meet the contemporary demand for auditing (applied knowledge) skills. Likewise, this will improve the company operational effectiveness including its governance, risk management, and compliance processes, financial stability and protecting the assets of the construction company in this new normal of modern business world.

Research Locale

The study will be conducted in Shanghai, China. Greenland Holdings Group Co., Ltd. is a globally operating mega conglomerate, founded on July 7, 1992, and headquartered in Shanghai, China. It is listed on the A-share market (18.SH) of China as a whole and holds a Hong Kong-listed company. Since its establishment 30 years ago, Greenland has formed a comprehensive business pattern with the "troika" of real estate, infrastructure, and finance as the core engines in the world and implemented a capitalization, publicization, and internationalization development strategy. Its development business has spread to more than 500 countries on five continents and has been listed in the Fortune Global 2022 for eleven consecutive years, ranking 125th.

Deeply cultivate China and lay out the world. Since 2013, Greenland Group has taken the lead in implementing the international development strategy, continuously upgrading the breadth and depth of overseas development, and widely deploying it in China, the United States, Australia, Canada, the United Kingdom, Japan, South Korea, Malaysia, and other countries, focusing on shaping the brand's international reputation and global competitiveness. Greenland aims to cultivate world-class companies and strives to achieve the unlimited future of Chinese businesses in the context of economic globalization.

Participants and Sampling Procedure

The respondents of the study will be the internal auditors and managers of a construction company in Shanghai, China.

The respondents will be selected through a non-probability sampling technique, in which the researcher makes choices based on the characteristics that a particular person possessed rather than randomly choosing from the population. Additionally, the purposive sampling method will be used, in which respondents are selected based on the qualities that the study requires. Thus, they are selected on purpose (Nikolopoulou, 2022).

According to Nikolopoulou (2022), non-probability sampling is a sampling technique that relies on factors other than randomness, such as the expert knowledge of the individuals that the researcher wants to investigate in order to find answers to their research questions.

The Greenland Real Estate Development Group, a construction company in Shanghai, China, will be the study's research locale.

At the present time, it is still unknown how many respondents made up the entire sample from the construction company. Based on the typical number of internal auditors and managers in a construction company in Shanghai, China, the number of respondents from the construction enterprise is represented in the table below. An audit team should typically have about 10% of the organization's total workforce as members (McDonald Consulting Group, 2023).

Table 1

The Research Locale of the Study

Construction Enterprise	Population		Sample Size		Percent	
	Internal Auditors	Managers	Internal Auditors	Managers	Internal Auditors	Managers
Greenland Real Estate Development Group. (Shanghai)	1295	555	223	96	70%	30%
Total	1850		319		100%	

The construction company has 10 branches, and a sample can be randomly selected from a population of 1850 individuals for this study. In this research, a confidence level of 95% and a margin of error of 5% were used, with a distribution of respondents set at 50%. By employing this sample size and distribution, the researcher can make inferences about the population with an appropriate level of confidence. Based on the calculations from the Sample Size Calculator, the total number of respondents for this study was determined to be 319 individuals.

Therefore, there will be a total of 319 respondents who will be asked to voluntarily participate in the research study in a construction company in Shanghai, China, based on the study's construction company's sample size, which includes managers and internal auditors.

Instrument of the Study

In this study, a self-made, validated research instrument based on the areas and sections of the Internal Audit Competency Framework of the Institute of Internal Auditors, supported by relevant theory and related studies.

The questionnaire will be divided into three parts for internal auditors (Parts 1 to 3), and two parts for managers (Parts 2 to 3) of the construction company.

Part I elicits items related to the profile of the internal auditors that include age, sex, educational attainment, and length of years at the company.

Part II elicits items related to the extent to which the internal audit practice is being implemented in a construction company. The sections include: audit professionalism; performance audit; operating environment; and leadership and communication. The respondents of the study will be asked to rate the extent to which the internal management audit practice is being implemented using a 4-point Likert rating scale, with 4 being interpreted as "fully implemented" and 1 being interpreted as "not implemented."

Part III elicits items related to the level of applied knowledge competency of the internal auditors. The areas of applied knowledge include professionalism, performance, environment, leadership, and communication. The respondents of the study will be asked to rate the level of applied knowledge competency of the members of the internal auditors of their respective construction enterprise using a 4-point Likert rating scale, with 4 being interpreted as "outstanding" and 1 being interpreted as "not competent."

Data Gathering Procedure

The instrument will go through content validation by the experts, which include an audit manager, an industry expert, and a university professor in the area of internal audit practices, before the pilot study is carried out.

The instrument of the study will be subject to a pilot study that will involve thirty (30) respondents composed of internal auditors and managers from another construction company in Shanghai, China. The actual data collection for the study will not involve the respondents in the pilot study. The outcomes of the pilot study will be tested for internal consistency using Cronbach's alpha to determine their reliability.

When the instrument has proven to be reliable, data collection can begin. A request letter will be emailed to the management of the construction company to ask for permission to conduct the study there. Upon receiving the management of the construction company's approval, the data collection process will begin.

In this study, the researcher will use an electronic questionnaire that will also go through face validation by the experts. Either a paper questionnaire or an online survey will be available to respondents.

Additionally, a letter requesting their voluntary participation in the study will also be included with the questionnaire. Upon receiving consent from the respondents of the chosen construction enterprise, the distribution of survey forms will start. If respondents have any concerns or queries about the instrument, the researcher will be available to address them. A week after the end of the data collection, the questionnaires will then be collected.

Ethical Considerations

The following ethical principles will be utilized throughout the course of the study:

The participants in the study will be asked for their consent. The gathering of data from them will begin once they agree to voluntarily participate in the study.

Moreover, in this study, it is the researcher's responsibility to fully disclose to the respondents the purpose, significance, and methodology of the research study. Before the study is conducted, their formal permission will be requested before the actual data collection.

Throughout the research, the right to self-determination will always be upheld as a fundamental principle. The study's respondents will be made aware that taking part is entirely voluntary and that they are permitted to discontinue at any time while data collection is still ongoing.

They will be told that taking part in the study may be beneficial to both as well as to the overall objective of the investigation. In addition, the study's respondents will be shielded from any influence of manipulation.

Also, the study will uphold its obligation to maintain confidentiality. This has to do with the researcher's responsibility to keep the data gathered from the study from being disclosed to others. Only research and related studies will make use of the data collected from the study.

The study will uphold the nameless principle, which pertains to anonymity. This is the practice of protecting the identities of the involved respondents from disclosure to third parties. When respondents agree to take part in the study, the researcher will make sure they are aware that no information they provide will ever be used to identify any participant.

Data Analysis and Statistical Treatment

The following statistical tools will be used to interpret and analyze the essential collected data from the study:

Frequency and Percentage Distribution

These will be utilized to determine the overall distribution of the profile of internal auditors as the primary respondents of the study that include age, sex, educational attainment, and length of years at the company. These will answer SOP 1.

Weighted Mean

This will be utilized to determine the extent to which the internal audit practices are being implemented by a construction company in Shanghai, China, in terms of the following sections: audit professionalism; performance audit; operating environment; and leadership and communication. This will answer SOP 2.

Moreover, weighted mean will be used to determine the level of applied knowledge competency of the internal auditors in a construction company in Shanghai, China, in terms of the following areas of applied knowledge: professionalism; performance; environment; leadership; and communication. This will answer SOP 3.

Table 2

Ratings Scale of the Extent to Which the Internal Audit Practices are Being Implemented

Scale	Range	Interpretation	Symbol
4	3.26-4.00	Fully Implemented	FI
3	2.51-3.25	Partially Implemented	PI
2	1.76-2.50	Less Implemented	LI
1	1.00-1.75	Not Implemented	NI

Table 2 presents the rating scale that will be utilized by the respondents to rate the extent to which the internal audit practices are being implemented by a construction company in terms of its sections.

Table 3

Rating Scale of the Level of Applied Knowledge Competencies of Internal Auditors

Scale	Range	Interpretation	Symbol
4	3.26-4.00	Outstanding	O
3	2.51-3.25	Competent	C
2	1.76-2.50	Less Competent	LC
1	1.00-1.75	Not Competent	NC

Table 3 presents the rating scale that will be utilized by the respondents to rate the level of competency of the internal auditors of the construction company in relation to the areas of applied knowledge.

Analysis of Variance (ANOVA)

This will be utilized to determine the significant difference in the assessments of the respondents in terms of the extent to which the internal audit practices are being implemented when grouped according to their profiles that include age, educational attainment, and length of years at the company. This will answer SOP 4.

Moreover, this will be utilized to determine the significant difference in the assessment of the respondents in terms of the level of competency of the internal auditors when grouped according to their profiles that include age, educational attainment, and length of years at the company.

Z-test

This will be utilized to determine the significant difference in the assessments of the respondents in terms of the extent to which the internal audit practices are being implemented when grouped according to their profiles that include sex. This will answer SOP 4.

Moreover, this will be utilized to determine the significant difference in the assessment of the respondents in terms of the level of competency of the internal auditors when grouped according to their profiles that include sex. This will answer SOP 5.

CHAPTER 3

RESULTS AND DISCUSSION

The chapter deals with the presentation of findings, analysis and interpretation of the data gathered by the researcher. The presentation is in tabular and textual forms to provide the readers a clearer insight to the results of the study.

The Profile of the Respondents

Table 4

The Profile of Internal Auditors

Profile Variables		Frequency	Percentage
Age			
21-30 years old		36	16.14
31-40 years old		126	56.50
41-50 years old		56	25.11
51 years old and above		5	2.24
	Total	**223**	**100.00**
Sex			
Male		91	40.81
Female		132	59.19
	Total	**223**	**100.00**

Educational Attainment

Bachelor's Degree		24	10.76
Master's Degree		168	75.34
Doctorate Degree		31	13.90
	Total	**223**	**100.00**

Length of Years at the Company

1-5 years		24	10.76
6-10 years		27	12.11
11-15 years		105	47.09
15-20 years		47	21.08
20-25 years		20	8.97
	Total	**223**	**100.00**

Table 4 shows the frequency and percentage distribution of the internal auditors in terms of their profiles.

As presented, 36 (16.14%) of the internal auditors as the primary respondents of the study are in the age group of 21-30 years old, 126 (56.50%) are in the age group of 31-40 years old, 56 (25.11%) are in the age group of 41-50 years old, and 5 (2.24%) are 51 years old and above.

In accordance with the sex groups, 91 (40.81%) are male internal auditors, whereas, 132 (59.19%) are females.

With their educational attainment, it shows that 24 (10.76%) are holders of Bachelor's Degree, 168 (75.34%) are graduates of master's degree, and 31 (13.90%) earned their doctorate degree.

Moreover, in terms of years at the company, 24 (10.76%) of the respondents are employed in the company for 1-5 years, 27 (12.11%) of them are 6-10 years, 105 (47.09%) of them are 11-15 years, 47 (21.08%) of them are 15-20 years, and 20 (8.97%) of them are 20-25 years.

As can be garnered from the table above, it reveals that most of the internal auditors who partook in the study from a construction company in Shanghai, China, are mostly between 31 to 40 years old, female internal auditors, with master's degree, and already 11-15 years in the company, whereas minority of them are 51 years old and older, male internal auditors, graduates of bachelor's degree, and who are employed for 20-25 years already.

Furthermore, this demonstrated that most internal auditors participated in the study who are between 31 to 40 years of age, mainly female, with graduate degrees, and who are senior internal auditors with more than a decade of experience in the company.

The Extent to Which the Internal Audit Practices are Being Implemented by a Construction Company in Shanghai, China, in Terms of the Sections

Audit Professionalism

Table 5

The Extent of Implementation of the Internal Audit Practices in Terms of Audit Professionalism

Audit Professionalism	Internal Auditors		Managers	
	WM	VI	WM	VI
1. Assess the internal audit activity's conformance with the internal auditors' code of ethics	2.97	PI	2.73	PI
2. Assess the competencies required to fulfill the responsibilities of the internal audit activity	3.02	PI	2.61	PI
3. Address any potential impairments to internal audit independence to achieve conformance with the standards	3.02	PI	2.66	PI
4. Review the internal audit activity's ability to conduct both assurance and consulting activities to add value and improve the company's operations.	3.12	PI	2.68	PI
5. Evaluate an internal audit charter to achieve conformance with the standards and promote world-class performance.	3.12	PI	2.73	PI

6. Develop policies that govern objectivity	3.14	PI	2.82	PI
7. Conclude on the application of due professional care	3.04	PI	2.80	PI
8. Recommend strategies to promote objectivity	3.20	PI	2.72	PI
9. Recommend strategies to promote the highest ethical standards for internal auditors and the internal audit activity	3.12	PI	2.75	PI
10. Promote professional development	3.06	PI	2.75	PI
Overall Mean	**3.08**	**PI**	**2.73**	**PI**

Legend: 3.26-4.00 (Fully Implemented-FI); 2.51-3.25 (Partially Implemented-PI); 1.76-2.50 (Less Implemented-LI); 1.00-1.75 (Not Implemented-NI)

Table 5 presents the extent to which the internal audit practices are being implemented by a construction company in Shanghai, China, in terms of audit professionalism utilizing weighted mean.

The collected data shows that item no. 8, with a weighted average score of 3.20 and verbally interpreted as partially implemented, as assessed by the internal auditors, obtained the highest weighted average score in terms of audit professionalism on the extent of implementation of internal audit practices, whereas item no. 1, with a weighted average score of 2.97 and verbally interpreted as partially implemented, obtained the lowermost mark.

In the assessment of managers, item no. 6, with a weighted average score of 2.82 and verbally interpreted as partially implemented received the highest weighted average score, whereas item no. 2, with a weighted average score of 2.61 and verbally interpreted as partially implemented received the lowermost mark.

Moreover, the extent to which the internal audit practices are being implemented by a construction company in Shanghai, China, in terms of audit professionalism as assessed by internal auditors and managers, respectively, received an overall mean of 3.08 and 2.73 both verbally interpreted as partially implemented.

Performance Audit

Table 6

The Extent of Implementation of the Internal Audit Practices in Terms of Performance Audit

Performance Audit	Internal Auditors		Managers	
	WM	**VI**	**WM**	**VI**
1. Assess the company's implementation of its internal control framework	3.05	PI	2.77	PI
2. Assess the audit engagement work program.	2.81	PI	2.52	PI
3. Apply scientific auditing techniques in fraud prevention, deterrence, and investigation	3.00	PI	2.58	PI
4. Appraise the methods used to assess the effectiveness of risk identification and management.	2.93	PI	2.56	PI
5. Evaluate the collective outcomes of	2.95	PI	2.53	PI
6. engagements performed by the internal	3.13	PI	2.67	PI
7. audit activity.	3.14	PI	2.64	PI
7. Evaluate monitoring and follow-up	3.08	PI	2.65	PI
9. performed by the internal audit activity	3.04	PI	2.76	PI
10. Evaluate analytical review techniques implemented during the audit engagement.	3.18	PI	2.69	PI
Overall Mean	**3.03**	**PI**	**2.64**	**PI**

Legend: 3.26-4.00 (Fully Implemented-FI); 2.51-3.25 (Partially Implemented-PI); 1.76-2.50 (Less Implemented-LI); 1.00-1.75 (Not Implemented-NI)

Table 6 presents the extent to which the internal audit practices are being implemented by a construction company in Shanghai, China, in terms of performance audit utilizing weighted mean.

The collected data shows that item no. 10, with a weighted average score of 3.18 and verbally interpreted as partially implemented, as assessed by the internal auditors, obtained the highest weighted average score in terms of performance audit on the extent of implementation of internal audit practices, whereas item no. 2, with a weighted average score of 2.81 and verbally interpreted as partially implemented, obtained the lowermost mark.

In the assessment of managers, item no. 1, with a weighted average score of 2.77 and verbally interpreted as partially implemented received the highest weighted average score, whereas item no. 2, with a weighted average score of 2.52 and verbally interpreted as partially implemented received the lowermost mark.

Moreover, the extent to which the internal audit practices are being implemented by a construction company in Shanghai, China, in terms of performance audit as assessed by internal auditors and managers, respectively, received an overall mean of 3.03 and 2.64 both verbally interpreted as partially implemented.

Operating Environment

Table 7

The Extent of Implementation of the Internal Audit Practices in Terms of Operating Environment

Operating Environment	Internal Auditors		Managers	
	WM	VI	WM	VI
1. Select appropriate performance measures.	3.10	PI	2.60	PI
2. Evaluate the use of data analytics and IT in auditing.	3.16	PI	2.56	PI
3. Evaluate financial statement accuracy and provide assurance.	3.15	PI	2.53	PI
4. Recommend improvements to the overall control environment and risk management strategy	3.24	PI	2.56	PI
5. Recommend improvements to the company's strategic planning process.	3.02	PI	2.59	PI

6. Recommend appropriate company behavior and performance management techniques.	3.31	FI	2.72	PI
7. Recommend actions to improve management's approach to leading and building company commitment.	2.97	PI	2.59	PI
8. Recommend actions to address risks related to the company's business processes	3.00	PI	2.65	PI
9. Recommend actions to improve the company's approach to social responsibility and sustainability	2.99	PI	2.75	PI
10. Recommend actions to address IT risks, information security, and data privacy.	3.12	PI	2.59	PI
Overall Mean	**3.11**	**PI**	**2.62**	**PI**

Legend: 3.26-4.00 (Fully Implemented-FI); 2.51-3.25 (Partially Implemented-PI); 1.76-2.50 (Less Implemented-LI); 1.00-1.75 (Not Implemented-NI)

Table 7 presents the extent to which the internal audit practices are being implemented by a construction company in Shanghai, China, in terms of operating environment utilizing weighted mean.

The collected data shows that item no. 6, with a weighted average score of 3.31 and verbally interpreted as fully implemented, as assessed by the internal auditors, obtained the highest weighted average score in terms of operating environment on the extent of implementation of internal audit practices, whereas item no. 7, with a weighted average score of 2.97 and verbally interpreted as partially implemented, obtained the lowermost mark.

In the assessment of managers, item no. 9, with a weighted average score of 2.75 and verbally interpreted as partially implemented received the highest weighted average score, whereas item no. 3, with a weighted average score of 2.53 and verbally interpreted as partially implemented received the lowermost mark.

Moreover, the extent to which the internal audit practices are being implemented by a construction company in Shanghai, China, in terms of operating environment as assessed by internal auditors and managers, respectively, received an overall mean of 3.11 and 2.62 both verbally interpreted as partially implemented.

Leadership and Communication

Table 8

The Extent of Implementation of the Internal Audit Practices in Terms of Leadership and Communication

Leadership and Communication	Internal Auditors		Managers	
	WM	VI	WM	VI
1. Assess the internal audit strategic plan.	3.13	PI	2.70	PI
2. Assess the talent management efforts of the internal audit activity.	3.13	PI	2.70	PI
3. Assess engagement supervision activities to ensure the quality of the internal audit activity.	3.02	PI	2.57	PI
4. Assess internal audit communications with stakeholders, including key performance indicators to evaluate the success of the internal audit activity, and recommend improvements.	3.20	PI	2.64	PI
5. Assess stakeholder relationships to achieve improvements.	3.11	PI	2.75	PI
6. Review policies, procedures, and administrative activities of the internal audit activity.	3.03	PI	2.69	PI
7. Coordinate assurance efforts with other providers to ensure proper coverage and minimize duplication of efforts.	3.04	PI	2.69	PI
8. Evaluate risk-based internal audit plan to meet the enterprise's evolving needs.	2.79	PI	2.71	PI
9. Evaluate the advocacy efforts of the internal audit activity.	2.99	PI	2.66	PI
10. Recommend improvements to the budget for the internal audit activity	2.91	PI	2.71	PI
Overall Mean	**3.03**	**PI**	**2.68**	**PI**

Legend: 3.26-4.00 (Fully Implemented-FI); 2.51-3.25 (Partially Implemented-PI); 1.76-2.50 (Less Implemented-LI); 1.00-1.75 (Not Implemented-NI)

Table 8 presents the extent to which the internal audit practices are being implemented by a construction company in Shanghai, China, in terms of leadership and communication utilizing weighted mean.

The collected data shows that item no. 4, with a weighted average score of 3.20 and verbally interpreted as partially implemented, as assessed by the internal auditors, obtained the highest weighted average score in terms of leadership and communication on the extent of implementation of internal audit practices, whereas item no. 8, with a weighted average score of 2.79 and verbally interpreted as partially implemented, obtained the lowermost mark.

In the assessment of managers, item no. 5, with a weighted average score of 2.75 and verbally interpreted as partially implemented received the highest weighted average score, whereas item no. 3, with a weighted average score of 2.57 and verbally interpreted as partially implemented received the lowermost mark.

Moreover, the extent to which the internal audit practices are being implemented by a construction company in Shanghai, China, in terms of leadership and communication as assessed by internal auditors and managers, respectively, received an overall mean of 3.03 and 2.68 both verbally interpreted as partially implemented.

Sections of Internal Audit Practices

Table 9

The Summary of the Extent of Implementation of the Internal Audit Practices in Terms of the Sections

Sections	Internal Auditors		Managers	
	WM	VI	WM	VI
1. Audit Professionalism	3.08	PI	2.73	PI
2. Performance Audit	3.03	PI	2.64	PI
3. Operating Environment	3.11	PI	2.62	PI
4. Leadership and Communication	3.03	PI	2.68	PI
Overall Mean	**3.06**	**PI**	**2.66**	**PI**

Legend: 3.26-4.00 (Fully Implemented-FI); 2.51-3.25 (Partially Implemented-PI); 1.76-2.50 (Less Implemented-LI); 1.00-1.75 (Not Implemented-NI)

Table 9 presents the extent to which the internal audit practices are being implemented by a construction company in Shanghai, China, in terms of sections utilizing weighted mean.

The collected data shows that item no. 3, with a weighted average score of 3.11 and verbally interpreted as partially implemented, as assessed by the internal auditors, obtained the highest weighted average score in terms of sections on the extent of implementation of internal audit practices, whereas items nos. 2 and 4, with a weighted average score of 3.03 and verbally interpreted as partially implemented, obtained the lowermost mark.

In the assessment of managers, item no. 1, with a weighted average score of 2.73 and verbally interpreted as partially implemented received the highest weighted average score, whereas item no. 3, with a weighted average score of 2.62 and verbally interpreted as partially implemented received the lowermost mark.

Moreover, the extent to which the internal audit practices are being implemented by a construction company in Shanghai, China, in terms of sections as assessed by internal auditors and managers, respectively, received an overall mean of 3.06 and 2.66 both verbally interpreted as partially implemented.

The Level of Applied Knowledge Competency of the Internal Auditors in a Construction Company in Shanghai, China, in Terms of the Areas of Applied Knowledge

Professionalism

Table 10

The Level of Applied Knowledge Competency of the Internal Auditor in Terms of Professionalism

Professionalism	Internal Auditors		Managers	
	WM	VI	WM	VI
1. Detect any potential impairments to internal audit independence and the impact.	2.94	C	2.54	C

2. Detect and manage any real or perceived impairments to an individual internal auditor's objectivity.	3.11	C	2.59	C
3. Prepare an internal audit charter in conformance with the standards and receive approval from the board.	3.10	C	2.67	C
4. Demonstrate ability to conduct both assurance and consulting engagements in conformance with the standards.	3.05	C	2.54	C
5. Demonstrate individual conformance with internal auditors' code of ethics.	3.00	C	2.58	C
6. Demonstrate due professional care.	3.17	C	2.70	C
7. Demonstrate internal audit competency through continuing professional development.	3.09	C	2.58	C
Overall Mean	**3.07**	**C**	**2.60**	**C**

Legend: 3.26-4.00 (Outstanding-O); 2.51-3.25 (Competent-C); 1.76-2.50 (Less Competent-LC); 1.00-1.75 (Not Competent-NC)

Table 10 presents the level of applied knowledge competency of the internal auditors in a construction company in Shanghai, China, in terms of professionalism utilizing weighted mean.

The collected data shows that item no. 6, with a weighted average score of 3.17 and verbally interpreted as competent, as assessed by the internal auditors, obtained the highest weighted average score in terms of professionalism on the level of applied knowledge competency of internal auditors, whereas item no. 1, with a weighted average score of 2.94 and verbally interpreted as competent, obtained the lowermost mark.

In the assessment of managers, item no. 6, with a weighted average score of 2.70 and verbally interpreted as competent received the highest weighted average score, whereas items nos. 1 and 4, with a weighted average score of 2.54 and verbally interpreted as competent received the lowermost mark.

Moreover, the level of applied knowledge competency of the internal auditors in a construction company in Shanghai, China, in terms of professionalism as assessed by internal auditors and managers, respectively, received an overall mean of 3.07 and 2.60 both verbally interpreted as competent.

Performance

Table 11

The Level of Applied Knowledge Competency of the Internal Auditor in Terms of Performance

Performance	Internal Auditors		Managers	
	WM	VI	WM	VI
1. Assess engagement outcomes, including the management action plan	3.15	C	2.57	C
2. Identify residual risk	3.13	C	2.56	C
3. Prepare an interim report; prepare a final audit report, seek approval, and distribute to appropriate parties.	3.24	C	2.73	C
4. Perform a preliminary survey of the engagement area, such as developing checklists and risk-and-control questionnaires, examining relevant information during an engagement, or the like.	3.01	C	2.70	C
5. Apply appropriate analytical approaches and process mapping techniques to evaluate the relevance, sufficiency, and reliability of potential sources of evidence	3.30	O	2.66	C
6. Formulate recommendations to enhance and protect enterprise value.	2.97	C	2.69	C
7. Manage monitoring and follow-up of the disposition of audit engagement results communicated to management and the board.	3.02	C	2.74	C
Overall Mean	**3.12**	**C**	**2.66**	**C**

Legend: 3.26-4.00 (Outstanding-O); 2.51-3.25 (Competent-C); 1.76-2.50 (Less Competent-LC); 1.00-1.75 (Not Competent-NC)

Table 11 presents the level of applied knowledge competency of the internal auditors in a construction company in Shanghai, China, in terms of performance utilizing weighted mean.

The collected data shows that item no. 5, with a weighted average score of 3.30 and verbally interpreted as outstanding, as assessed by the internal auditors, obtained the highest weighted average score in terms of performance on the level of applied knowledge competency of internal auditors, whereas item no. 6, with a weighted average score of 2.97 and verbally interpreted as competent, obtained the lowermost mark.

In the assessment of managers, item no. 7, with a weighted average score of 2.74 and verbally interpreted as competent received the highest weighted average score, whereas item no. 2, with a weighted average score of 2.56 and verbally interpreted as competent received the lowermost mark.

Moreover, the level of applied knowledge competency of the internal auditors in a construction company in Shanghai, China, in terms of performance as assessed by internal auditors and managers, respectively, received an overall mean of 3.12 and 2.66 both verbally interpreted as competent.

Environment

Table 12

The Level of Applied Knowledge Competency of the Internal Auditor in Terms of Environment

Environment	Internal Auditors		Managers	
	WM	VI	WM	VI
1. Examine management's effectiveness to lead and build company commitment.	3.02	C	2.63	C
2. Examine the risks and controls related to the company's business processes.	3.12	C	2.53	C
3. Examine the organization's approach to social responsibility and sustainability	3.12	C	2.66	C
4. Apply data analytics and IT in auditing, such as identifying and assessing various risks related to IT, information security, and data privacy.	3.14	C	2.58	C
5. Conduct financial analyses and interpret financial statements.	3.04	C	2.57	C

6. Analyze the company's strategic planning process	3.20	C	2.55	C
7. Evaluate the company's governance structure and the impact of organizational structure and culture on the overall control environment and risk management strategy.	3.12	C	2.60	C
Overall Mean	**3.11**	**C**	**2.59**	**C**

Legend: 3.26-4.00 (Outstanding-O); 2.51-3.25 (Competent-C); 1.76-2.50 (Less Competent-LC); 1.00-1.75 (Not Competent-NC)

Table 12 presents the level of applied knowledge competency of the internal auditors in a construction company in Shanghai, China, in terms of environment utilizing weighted mean.

The collected data shows that item no. 6, with a weighted average score of 3.20 and verbally interpreted as competent, as assessed by the internal auditors, obtained the highest weighted average score in terms of environment on the level of applied knowledge competency of internal auditors, whereas item no. 1, with a weighted average score of 3.02 and verbally interpreted as competent, obtained the lowermost mark.

In the assessment of managers, item no. 3, with a weighted average score of 2.66 and verbally interpreted as competent received the highest weighted average score, whereas item no. 2, with a weighted average score of 2.53 and verbally interpreted as competent received the lowermost mark.

Moreover, the level of applied knowledge competency of the internal auditors in a construction company in Shanghai, China, in terms of environment as assessed by internal auditors and managers, respectively, received an overall mean of 3.11 and 2.59 both verbally interpreted as competent.

Leadership

Table 13

The Level of Applied Knowledge Competency of the Internal Auditor in Terms of Leadership

Leadership	Internal Auditors		Managers	
	WM	VI	WM	VI
1. Conduct a risk assessment, prioritize engagements, develop a risk-based internal audit plan, and obtain board approval.	3.06	C	2.44	LC
2. Prepare a risk assurance map.	3.05	C	2.41	LC
3. Schedule and complete internal quality assessment to meet requirements and report results.	2.81	C	2.59	C
4. Create the internal audit strategic plan in alignment with the company's strategy, risk profile, and risk management strategy.	3.00	C	2.42	LC
5. Create policies and procedures for managing internal audit operations.	2.93	C	2.44	LC
6. Create an effective and efficient budget for the internal audit activity	2.95	C	2.50	LC
7. Formulate appropriate disclosures of conformance vs. nonconformance with the standards.	3.13	C	2.47	LC
Overall Mean	**2.99**	**C**	**2.47**	**LC**

Legend: 3.26-4.00 (Outstanding-O); 2.51-3.25 (Competent-C); 1.76-2.50 (Less Competent-LC); 1.00-1.75 (Not Competent-NC)

Table 13 presents the level of applied knowledge competency of the internal auditors in a construction company in Shanghai, China, in terms of leadership utilizing weighted mean.

The collected data shows that item no. 7, with a weighted average score of 3.13 and verbally interpreted as competent, as assessed by the internal auditors, obtained the highest weighted average score in terms of leadership on the level of applied knowledge competency of internal auditors, whereas item no. 3, with a weighted average score of 2.81 and verbally interpreted as competent, obtained the lowermost mark.

In the assessment of managers, item no. 3, with a weighted average score of 2.59 and verbally interpreted as competent received the highest weighted average score, whereas item no. 2, with a weighted average score of 2.41 and verbally interpreted as less competent received the lowermost mark.

Moreover, the level of applied knowledge competency of the internal auditors in a construction company in Shanghai, China, in terms of leadership received an overall mean of 2.99 and 2.47 and verbally interpreted as competent for internal auditors' and less competent for managers' assessments.

Communication

Table 14

The Level of Applied Knowledge Competency of the Internal Auditor in Terms of Communication

Communication	Internal Auditors		Managers	
	WM	VI	WM	VI
1. Detect opportunities for change and facilitate change	3.14	C	2.66	C
2. Prepare relevant and appropriate communications for internal audit stakeholders, including reports to senior management and the board (e.g., significant risk exposures, key performance indicators, etc.)	3.08	C	2.55	C
3. Demonstrate sincerity, honesty, and empathy in communications with stakeholders to build trust and maintain relationships.	3.04	C	2.67	C
4. Demonstrate soft skills (conflict management, influence, and persuasion)	3.18	C	2.60	C
5. Provide insightful consultation to contribute to the	3.10	C	2.64	C
6. company's effectiveness	3.16	C	2.66	C

7. Recommend actions to achieve improvements on stakeholder relationships.	3.15	C	2.68	C
Overall Mean	**3.12**	**C**	**2.64**	**C**

Legend: 3.26-4.00 (Outstanding-O); 2.51-3.25 (Competent-C); 1.76-2.50 (Less Competent-LC); 1.00-1.75 (Not Competent-NC)

Table 14 presents the level of applied knowledge competency of the internal auditors in a construction company in Shanghai, China, in terms of communication utilizing weighted mean.

The collected data shows that item no. 4, with a weighted average score of 3.18 and verbally interpreted as competent, as assessed by the internal auditors, obtained the highest weighted average score in terms of communication on the level of applied knowledge competency of internal auditors, whereas item no. 3, with a weighted average score of 3.04 and verbally interpreted as competent, obtained the lowermost mark.

In the assessment of managers, item no. 7, with a weighted average score of 2.68 and verbally interpreted as competent received the highest weighted average score, whereas item no. 2, with a weighted average score of 2.55 and verbally interpreted as competent received the lowermost mark.

Moreover, the level of applied knowledge competency of the internal auditors in a construction company in Shanghai, China, in terms of communication as assessed by internal auditors and managers, respectively, received an overall mean of 3.12 and 2.64 both verbally interpreted as competent.

Areas of Applied Knowledge

Table 15

The Summary of the Level of Applied Knowledge Competency of the Internal Auditor in Terms of the areas of applied knowledge

Areas of Applied Knowledge	Internal Auditors		Managers	
	WM	VI	WM	VI
1. Professionalism	3.07	C	2.60	C
2. Performance	3.12	C	2.66	C

3. Environment	3.11	C	2.59	C
4. Leadership	2.99	C	2.47	LC
5. Communication	3.12	C	2.64	C
Overall Mean	**3.08**	**C**	**2.59**	**C**

Legend: 3.26-4.00 (Outstanding-O); 2.51-3.25 (Competent-C); 1.76-2.50 (Less Competent-LC); 1.00-1.75 (Not Competent-NC)

Table 15 presents the level of applied knowledge competency of the internal auditors in a construction company in Shanghai, China, in terms of the areas of applied knowledge utilizing weighted mean.

The collected data shows that items nos. 2 and 5, with a weighted average score of 3.12 and verbally interpreted as competent, as assessed by the internal auditors, obtained the highest weighted average score in terms of the areas on the level of applied knowledge competency of internal auditors, whereas item no. 4, with a weighted average score of 2.99 and verbally interpreted as competent, obtained the lowermost mark.

In the assessment of managers, item no. 2, with a weighted average score of 2.66 and verbally interpreted as competent received the highest weighted average score, whereas item no. 4, with a weighted average score of 2.47 and verbally interpreted as less competent received the lowermost mark.

Moreover, the level of applied knowledge competency of the internal auditors in a construction company in Shanghai, China, in terms of the areas of applied knowledge as assessed by internal auditors and managers, respectively, received an overall mean of 3.08 and 2.59 both verbally interpreted as competent.

The Significant Difference in the Assessments of the Respondents in Terms of the Extent to Which the Internal Audit Practices are Being Implemented When Grouped According to Their Profiles

Age

Table 16

The Significant Difference in the Assessments of the Respondents in Terms of the Extent of Implementation of the Internal Audit Practices When Grouped According to Age

Age	Mean	SD	Computed Value	p	Decision	Interpretation
21-30 years old	2.73	0.14				
31-40 years old	3.16	0.13				
41-50 years old	3.05	0.16	$F = 47.75$	0.000	Reject Ho	Significant
51 years old and above	3.06	0.23				

Table 16 shows the significant difference in the assessments of the respondents in terms of the extent to which the internal audit practices are being implemented when grouped according to their age utilizing analysis of variance (ANOVA).

As can be garnered from the table, the computed p-value (0.000) is lesser than 0.05 alpha's level of significance, which specified a decision for rejection of the null hypothesis. This implied that there is adequate indication to conclude that there is a significant difference in the responses of internal auditors as quantified from the age groups.

Moreover, from the computed averages, internal auditors who are 31-40 years old assessed the implementation of internal audit practices in greater aspect as compared to other groups. It can also observe that respondents from the age group 21-30 years old had assessed the implementation on the least degree. This identified distinctions could be used in order to continuously enhance the implementation of internal audit practices in the construction company.

Therefore, there is a significant difference the significant difference in the assessments of the respondents in terms of the extent to which the internal audit practices are being implemented when they were grouped according to age.

Sex

Table 17

The Significant Difference in the Assessments of the Respondents in Terms of the Extent of Implementation of the Internal Audit Practices When Grouped According to Sex

Sex	Mean	SD	Computed Value	p	Decision	Interpretation
Male	2.92	0.11	$z = 10.94$	0.000	Reject Ho	Significant
Female	3.27	0.16				

Table 17 shows the significant difference in the assessments of the respondents in terms of the extent to which the internal audit practices are being implemented when grouped according to their sex utilizing z-test.

As can be garnered from the table, the computed p-value (0.000) is lesser than 0.05 alpha's level of significance, which specified a decision for rejection of the null hypothesis. This implied that there is adequate indication to conclude that there is a significant difference in the responses of internal auditors as quantified from the sex groups.

Moreover, from the computed averages, internal auditors who are female assessed the implementation of internal audit practices in greater aspect as compared to male group. This identified dissimilarities in the demographics from each sex group could be used in order to continuously enhance the implementation of internal audit practices in the construction company.

Therefore, there is a significant difference the significant difference in the assessments of the respondents in terms of the extent to which the internal audit practices are being implemented when they were grouped according to sex.

Educational Attainment

Table 18

The Significant Difference in the Assessments of the Respondents in Terms of the Extent of Implementation of the Internal Audit Practices When Grouped According to Educational Attainment

Educational Attainment	Mean	SD	Computed Value	p	Decision	Interpretation
Bachelor's Degree	3.09	0.14				
Master's Degree	3.13	0.13	$F = 108.44$	0.000	Reject Ho	Significant
Doctorate Degree	2.66	0.20				

Table 18 shows the significant difference in the assessments of the respondents in terms of the extent to which the internal audit practices are being implemented when grouped according to their educational attainment utilizing analysis of variance (ANOVA).

As can be garnered from the table, the computed p-value (0.000) is lesser than 0.05 alpha's level of significance, which specified a decision for rejection of the null hypothesis. This implied that there is adequate indication to conclude that there is a significant difference in the responses of internal auditors as quantified from the educational attainment groups.

Moreover, from the computed averages, internal auditors who are master's degree holders assessed the implementation of internal audit practices in greater aspect as compared to other groups. It can also observe that respondents from the internal auditors who earned their doctorate degree had assessed the implementation on the least degree. This identified dissimilarities in the demographics could be used in order to continuously enhance the implementation of internal audit practices in the construction company.

Therefore, there is a significant difference the significant difference in the assessments of the respondents in terms of the extent to which the internal audit practices are being implemented when they were grouped according to educational attainment.

Length of Years at the Company

Table 19

The Significant Difference in the Assessments of the Respondents in Terms of the Extent of Implementation of the Internal Audit Practices When Grouped According to Length of Years at the Company

Length of Years at the Company	Mean	SD	Computed Value	p	Decision	Interpretation
1-5 years	2.67	0.17				
6-10 years	3.14	0.17				
11-15 years	3.13	0.14	$F = 53.16$	0.000	Reject Ho	Significant
15-20 years	3.09	0.12				
20-25 years	2.99	0.23				

Table 19 shows the significant difference in the assessments of the respondents in terms of the extent to which the internal audit practices are being implemented when grouped according to their length of years at the company utilizing analysis of variance (ANOVA).

As can be garnered from the table, the computed p-value (0.000) is lesser than 0.05 alpha's level of significance, which specified a decision for rejection of the null hypothesis. This implied that there is adequate indication to conclude that there is a significant difference in the responses of internal auditors as quantified from the length of years at the company groups.

Moreover, from the computed averages, internal auditors who are in the company for 6 to 15 years assessed the implementation of internal audit practices in greater aspects as compared to other groups. It can also observe that respondents who were in their early stage of their career in the company had assessed the implementation on the least degree. This identified differences in the demographics could be used in order to continuously enhance the implementation of internal audit practices in the construction company.

Therefore, there is a significant difference the significant difference in the assessments of the respondents in terms of the extent to which the internal audit practices are being implemented when they were grouped according to length of years at the company.

The Significant Difference in the Assessment of the Respondents in Terms of the Level of Competency of the Internal Auditors When Grouped According to Their Profiles

Age

Table 20

The Significant Difference in the Assessments of the Respondents in Terms of the Level of Competency of the Internal Auditors When Grouped According to Age

Age	Mean	SD	Computed Value	p	Decision	Interpretation
21-30 years old	2.74	0.18				
31-40 years old	3.17	0.12				
41-50 years old	3.10	0.15	$F = 39.86$	0.000	Reject Ho	Significant
51 years old and above	2.93	0.25				

Table 20 shows the significant difference in the assessments of the respondents in terms of the level of competency of the internal auditors when grouped according to age utilizing analysis of variance (ANOVA).

From the computed gathered data shown in the table, the p-value (0.000) is lesser than 0.05 alpha's level of significance, which specified a decision for rejection of the null hypothesis. This implied that there is adequate indication to conclude that there is a significant difference in the responses of internal auditors as measured from the age groups.

Furthermore, from the computed means, internal auditors who are 31-40 years old perceived their level of competency in better level as compared to other groups. It can also observe that respondents from the 21-30 years had assessed their competency on the least degree. This identified gaps in the demographics could be used in order to continuously enhance the perceived level of competency of internal audit practices in the construction company.

Therefore, there is a significant difference in the assessments of the respondents in terms of the level of competency of the internal auditors when grouped according to age.

Sex

Table 21

The Significant Difference in the Assessments of the Respondents in Terms of the Level of Competency of the Internal Auditors When Grouped According to Sex

Sex	Mean	SD	Computed Value	p	Decision	Interpretation
Male	3.31	0.17	$z = 11.61$	0.000	Reject Ho	Significant
Female	2.92	0.09				

Table 21 shows the significant difference in the assessments of the respondents in terms of the level of competency of the internal auditors when grouped according to sex utilizing z-test.

From the computed gathered data shown in the table, the p-value (0.000) is lesser than 0.05 alpha's level of significance, which specified a decision for rejection of the null hypothesis. This implied that there is adequate indication to conclude that there is a significant difference in the responses of internal auditors as measured from the sex groups.

Furthermore, from the computed means, internal auditors who are male perceived their level of competency in better level as compared to female group. This distinction on the identified gap in the demographics could be used in order to continuously enhance the perceived level of competency of internal audit practices in the construction company.

Therefore, there is a significant difference in the assessments of the respondents in terms of the level of competency of the internal auditors when grouped according to sex.

Educational Attainment

Table 22

The Significant Difference in the Assessments of the Respondents in Terms of the Level of Competency of the Internal Auditors When Grouped According to Educational Attainment

Educational Attainment	Mean	SD	Computed Value	p	Decision	Interpretation
Bachelor's Degree	3.14	0.16				
Master's Degree	3.15	0.12	$F = 85.62$	0.000	Reject Ho	Significant
Doctorate Degree	2.68	0.22				

Table 22 shows the significant difference in the assessments of the respondents in terms of the level of competency of the internal auditors when grouped according to educational attainment utilizing analysis of variance (ANOVA).

From the computed gathered data shown in the table, the *p*-value (0.000) is lesser than 0.05 alpha's level of significance, which specified a decision for rejection of the null hypothesis. This implied that there is adequate indication to conclude that there is a significant difference in the responses of internal auditors as measured from the educational attainment groups.

Furthermore, from the computed means, internal auditors who are master's degree holders perceived their level of competency in better level as compared to other groups. It can also observe that respondents with doctorate degrees had assessed their competency on the least mark. This identified distinction in the demographics could be used in order to continuously enhance the perceived level of competency of internal audit practices in the construction company.

Therefore, there is a significant difference in the assessments of the respondents in terms of the level of competency of the internal auditors when grouped according to educational attainment.

Length of Years at the Company

Table 23

The Significant Difference in the Assessments of the Respondents in Terms of the Level of Competency of the Internal Auditors When Grouped According to Length of Years at the Company

Length of Years at the Company	Mean	SD	Computed Value	*p*	Decision	Interpretation
1-5 years	2.68	0.23				
6-10 years	3.15	0.22				
11-15 years	3.15	0.13	$F = 36.90$	0.000	Reject Ho	Significant
15-20 years	3.10	0.12				
20-25 years	3.02	0.23				

Table 23 shows the significant difference in the assessments of the respondents in terms of the level of competency of the internal auditors when grouped according to length of years at the company utilizing analysis of variance (ANOVA).

From the computed gathered data shown in the table, the *p*-value (0.000) is lesser than 0.05 alpha's level of significance, which specified a decision for rejection of the null hypothesis. This implied that there is adequate indication to conclude that there is a significant difference in the responses of internal auditors as measured from the length of years at the company groups.

Furthermore, from the computed means, internal auditors who are in the company for 6 to 15 years perceived their level of competency in better level as compared to other groups. It can also observe that respondents who are in their early stage of their career and those internal auditors who are approaching 25 years in the company had assessed their competency on a lesser degree. This identified distinctions in the perceptions of the capability based on the demographics could be used in order to continuously enhance the perceived level of competency of internal audit practices in the construction company across length of years at the company.

Therefore, there is a significant difference in the assessments of the respondents in terms of the level of competency of the internal auditors when grouped according to length of years at the company.

Summary of the Findings

After a thorough analysis and interpretation of the gathered data, the researcher drawn the following general findings:

1. The overall distributions of the profile of the respondents were determined according to the following:

    1.1 In terms of age, most of the internal auditors are between 31 to 40 years old, whereas minority of them are 51 years old and older.

    1.2 In terms of sex, most of the internal auditors are females, whereas minority of them are males.

    1.3 In terms of educational attainment, most of the internal auditors are holders of master's degree, whereas minority of them are graduates of bachelor's degree.

    1.4 In terms of years at the company, most of the internal auditors are already 11-15 years in the company, whereas minority of them are employed for 20-25 years already.

2. The extent to which the internal audit practices are being implemented by a construction company in Shanghai, China was assessed according to the following by the themselves and managers, respectively:

    2.1 In terms of audit professionalism, the extent of internal audit practices' implementation received an overall mean of 3.08 and 2.73 both verbally interpreted as partially implemented.

    2.2 In terms of performance audit, the extent of internal audit practices' implementation received an overall mean of 3.03 and 2.64 both verbally interpreted as partially implemented.

    2.3 In terms of operating environment, the extent of internal audit practices' implementation received an overall mean of 3.11 and 2.62 both verbally interpreted as partially implemented.

    2.4 In terms of leadership and communication, the extent of internal audit practices' implementation received an overall mean of 3.03 and 2.68 both verbally interpreted as partially implemented.

3. The level of applied knowledge competency of the internal auditors in a construction company in Shanghai, China, was assessed according to the following by the themselves and managers, respectively:

    3.1 In terms of professionalism, the level of applied knowledge competency of the internal auditors received an overall mean of 3.07 and 2.60 both verbally interpreted as competent.

    3.2 In terms of performance, the level of applied knowledge competency of the internal auditors received an overall mean of 3.12 and 2.66 both verbally interpreted as competent.

    3.3 In terms of environment, the level of applied knowledge competency of the internal auditors received an overall mean of 3.11 and 2.59 both verbally interpreted as competent.

    3.4 In terms of leadership, the level of applied knowledge competency of the internal auditors received an overall mean of 2.99 and 2.47 and verbally interpreted as competent for internal auditors' and less competent for managers' assessments.

    3.5 In terms of communication, the level of applied knowledge competency of the internal auditors received an overall mean of 3.12 and 2.64 both verbally interpreted as competent.

4. The significant difference in the assessments of the respondents in terms of the extent to which the internal audit practices are being implemented when they were grouped according to their profiles revealed the following:

    4.1 In terms of age, the computed p-value (0.000) is lesser than 0.05 alpha's level of significance, which specified a decision for rejection of the null hypothesis.

    4.2 In terms of sex, the computed p-value (0.000) is lesser than 0.05 alpha's level of significance, which specified a decision for rejection of the null hypothesis.

    4.3 In terms of educational attainment, the computed p-value (0.000) is lesser than 0.05 alpha's level of significance, which specified a decision for rejection of the null hypothesis.

    4.4 In terms of length of years at the company, the computed p-value (0.000) is lesser than 0.05 alpha's level of significance, which specified a decision for rejection of the null hypothesis.

5. The significant difference in the assessment of the respondents in terms of the level of competency of the internal auditors when they were grouped according to their profiles revealed the following:

    5.1 In terms of age, the computed p-value (0.000) is lesser than 0.05 alpha's level of significance, which specified a decision for rejection of the null hypothesis

    5.2 In terms of sex, the computed p-value (0.000) is lesser than 0.05 alpha's level of significance, which specified a decision for rejection of the null hypothesis.

    5.3 In terms of educational attainment, the computed p-value (0.000) is lesser than 0.05 alpha's level of significance, which specified a decision for rejection of the null hypothesis.

    5.4 In terms of length of years at the company, the computed p-value (0.000) is lesser than 0.05 alpha's level of significance, which specified a decision for rejection of the null hypothesis.

Conclusions

Based on the findings of the study, the researcher has drawn the following conclusions

1. Most internal auditors who participated in the study are between 31 to 40 years of age, mainly female, have graduate degrees, and are senior internal auditors with more than a decade of experience in the company.

2. According to the internal audit practices' findings, the most extensively employed sections were operating environment and audit professionalism. Although the results indicated reasonable implementation, there were still inadequacies in the leadership and communication, and performance audit. To completely carry out internal audit practice standards and fulfill business objectives, the company should take the findings into consideration.

3. Overall, it was determined that internal auditors' level of applied knowledge competency was satisfactory. It was discovered that internal auditors are capable enough regarding their overall audit performance. However, it was discovered that it was crucial for internal auditors to fully comprehend their environment and develop their leadership abilities. It is necessary to consider about how they may convey the outcomes

of their audit in a manner that is respectful of professionalism. These results need to be taken as a basis by the business to continue training internal auditors and putting their skills into effect in achieving goals for the company.

4.   The study concluded that there is a significant difference in the assessments of the respondents (internal auditors and managers) in terms of the extent to which the internal audit practices are being implemented when grouped according to their profiles.

5.   The study concluded that there is a significant difference in the assessment of the respondents (internal auditors and managers) in terms of the level of competency of the internal auditors when grouped according to their profiles.

Recommendations

The researcher proposed the following recommendations based on the general findings and conclusions of the study:

1.   It is recommended for future studies to include a qualitative data gathering process in order to have an in-extensive understanding of the issues and concerns surrounding internal auditing practices.

2.   Future studies may also include external auditors among the respondents to have a broader scope of the research results.

3.   The present study recommends including other variables that may improve the findings of the investigation and build up broader results from the limitations of the study, such as accounting systems and external control.

4.   From the results of applied competencies, the internal auditors need to possess and develop their knowledge and skills through appropriate professional training and development continuously and collectively. The training and development program should be improved on a regular basis and updated according to the latest developments in internal auditing.

5.   A proposed action plan for the construction company to enhance its processes for internal auditing is provided below.

Proposed Action Plan for the Construction Company to Improve Its Internal Audit Practices

General Objective:

For internal auditors to remain relevant, they must adapt to changing expectations and maintain alignment with organizational objectives.

Specific Objectives:

1. demonstrate competence and due professional care

2. demonstrate quality and continuous improvement.

3. provide internal auditors with the communication skills needed for successful internal auditing.

4. demonstrate insightful, proactive, and future-focused leadership skills

5. promote company improvement

The proposed action plan aims to provide *a series of training and development opportunities* for internal auditors on the following areas of concern:

Areas of Concern	Activities for Training and Development
Enhancing Internal Auditors' Leadership Skills	The construction company's management should offer internal auditors a leadership development program that focuses on their leadership roles, which call for the capacity to identify and navigate the differences in professional relationships, identify the company's systems and culture's strengths and weaknesses, as well as place themselves in highly effective positions. The development of internal auditors' leadership abilities should be a deliberate, self-reflective, and proactive part of this program.

Improving Internal Auditors' Communication Skills	The internal auditors should be able to recognize and comprehend the various interpersonal communication strategies. Effective communication skills should be used by internal auditors in practically every circumstance. The internal auditors must convey the idea that they are contributing to the business and are not merely conducting investigations. When working with various types of people at various levels inside the company, internal auditors must have excellent listening and interpersonal skills as well as be vigilant and mindful when utilizing certain language reflections. Internal auditors need to be conscious of how their demeanor affects auditees.
Up-To-Date Knowledge	The internal audit profession is no exception to the dynamic nature of the business world. Internal auditors should receive regular training to ensure they have the most up-to-date information and abilities necessary to perform their jobs effectively and efficiently.
Enhance Compliance with Standards	The internal auditors are expected to adhere to global standards established by professional organizations as well as national standards established by the government. The construction company should continue providing internal auditors with training and development, particularly in terms of recognizing these standards, in order to enable them achieve the expectations of their profession as well as the overall business objectives.

Improve Internal Audit Performance Quality	Internal auditors' abilities and knowledge determine the quality of an audit's outcome. Regular quality assurance training ensures that internal auditors have the skills and information needed to undertake high-quality audits.
Increase Internal Auditors Efficiency	Internal auditor training supports them in improving their audit processes and procedures, making them more efficient and effective. This can result in savings on expenditures for the company. To increase internal auditors' efficiency, the training may concentrate on organizational governance, risk management, internal control, and analytical evaluation.
Career Development	Internal audit profession training should be conducted on a regular basis by the company in order to provide opportunity for internal auditors to expand their skills and knowledge, which can lead to career advancement within the profession and help the business achieve its goals.

Persons Involved

1. Internal Auditors
2. Management
3. Heads of the Concerned Departments
4. Audit Committee

Expected Outcomes

1. The foundation for relying on internal auditors' judgment is trust, which is established through their integrity.
2. The highest level of professional objectivity is displayed by internal auditors when they gather, assess, and communicate data concerning the activity or process under scrutiny.

3. Internal auditors develop decisions based on a fair evaluation of all the pertinent facts without being excessively swayed by personal or outside interests.

4. Internal auditors respect the ownership and value of the information they are given, and they never divulge information without proper authorization unless there is a legal or ethical requirement to do so.

5. Internal auditors use their expertise, knowledge, and experience to perform internal audit services.

REFERENCES

Abdullahi, R., & Mansor, N. (2015). Forensic accounting and frauds risk factors: The influence of fraud diamond theory. *The American Journal of Innovative Research and Applied Sciences, 1*(5), 186-192.

Alqudah, H., Amran, N., & Hassan, H. (2019). Factors affecting the internal auditors' effectiveness in the Jordanian public sector. *EuroMed Journal of Business, 14,* 251–73.

Barišić, I., & Tušek, B. (2016). The importance of the supportive control environment for internal audit effectiveness – the case of Croatian companies. *Economic Research-Ekonomska Istraživanja, 29*(1), 1021-1037. https://doi.org/10.1080/1331677X.2016.1211954

Behrend, J., & Eulerich, M. (2019). The evolution of internal audit research: A bibliometric analysis of published documents (1926–2016). *Accounting History Review, 29,* 103–39.

Cao, Y., & Zhang, W. (2020). Analysis of Internal Audit Management of Construction Enterprises in China under the Background of Industry 4.0. Journal of Modern Accounting and Auditing, 16(2), 51-57.

Cao, Y., & Zhang, W. (2020). Analysis of Internal Audit Management of Construction Enterprises in China under the Background of Industry 4.0. Journal of Modern Accounting and Auditing, 16(2), 51-57.

Chambers, A. D., & Odar, M. (2015). A new vision for internal audit. *Managerial Auditing Journal, 30*(1), 34-55.

Chen, L., & Li, X. (2019). Ethical culture, internal audit effectiveness, and compliance with regulations: Evidence from China. *Journal of Business Ethics, 156*(3), 647-661.

Chen, Y., & Li, Y. (2019). Ethics, internal audit quality, and corporate governance in China. *Journal of Business Ethics, 155*(1), 257-274.

Competency-Based Framework for Internal Auditors. (2021). *Central coordinating agency for internal audit service.* Ministry of Finance. https://www.rcsc.gov.bt/wp-content/uploads/2021/11/Internal-Auditor-.pdf

Deloitte. (2021). *COVID-19: Implications for internal audit.* https://www2. deloitte.com/us/en/insights/economy/covid-19/covid-19-internal-audit-implications.html

Dwi, C., & Effendi, D. (2013). *Pengaruh profesionalisme akuntan forensik terhadap kompetensi bukti tindak pidana korupsi* (Studi kasus di badan pemeriksa keuangan dan pengembangan Provinsi Jawa Barat).

Dzikrullah, A. D., Harymawan, I., Ratri, M. C., & Ntim, C. G. (2020) Internal audit functions and audit outcomes: Evidence from Indonesia, *Cogent Business & Management, 7*(1). https://doi.org/10.1080/23311975.2020.1 750331

Eisenhardt, K. M. (1989). Agency theory: An assessment and review. *The Academy of Management Review, 14*(1), 57-74. https://doi. org/10.2307/258191

Endaya, H. A., & Hanefah, M. M. (2013). Internal audit effectiveness: An approach proposition to develop the theoretical framework. *Research Journal of Finance and Accounting, 4*(10).

Endaya, K., & Hanefah, M. (2016). Internal auditor characteristics, internal audit effectiveness, and moderating effect of senior management. *Journal of Economic and Administrative Sciences, 32*, 160–76.

Eulerich, M., Kremin, J., & David, A. Wood. 2019. Factors that influence the perceived use of the internal audit function's work by executive management and audit committee. *Advances in Accounting, 45*, 100410.

Farnham, K. (2021, November 24). *7 Strategies for effective internal audit management.* Diligent. https://www.diligent.com/insights/grc/internal-audit-management/

Francis, T. M. (2022, March 23). 5 top challenges for internal auditors. Wipfli. https://www.wipfli.com/insights/articles/ra-5-top-challenges-for-internal-auditors

Gartner. (2022). *Gartner Survey Reveals the Top Challenges for Internal Audit in 2022.* https://www.gartner.com/en/newsroom/press-releases/2022-03-17-gartner-survey-reveals-the-top-challenges-for-internal-audit-in-2022

Gurama, Z., Sani., A. A., & Hammayo, A. A. (2019). Communication as a critical factor for internal audit effectiveness in tax administration in Nigeria. *International Journal of Business and Technopreneurship, 9*(1), 103-112.

He, H., & Chen, H. (2019). Research on the application of technology in internal audit management in China. *Journal of Intelligence, 38*(4), 64-70.

He, X., & Chen, Y. (2019). Technology-enabled internal audit in China: Challenges and opportunities. *Managerial Auditing Journal, 34*(7), 762-774.

Heyrani, F., Banimahd, B., & Roudposhti, F. R. (2016). Investigation of the effect of auditors' professionalism levels on their judgment to resolve the conflict between auditor and management. *Procedia Economics and Finance, 36*, 177-188. https://doi.org/10.1016/S2212-5671(16)30029-6.

Li, C., & Li, Z. (2018). Risk management and internal audit in China: An exploratory study. *Journal of Accounting in Emerging Economies, 8*(3), 366-382.

Li, E., Xu, H., & Li, G. (2020). Analysis on improvement of internal audit in China's listed companies based on artificial intelligence. *Advances in Economics, Business and Management Research, 133*, 25-30. http://creativecommons.org/licenses/by-nc/4.0/.

Li, L., Zhang, H., & Wei, L. (2021). The role of internal audit in the risk management of construction enterprises in China. *Journal of Risk Analysis and Crisis Response, 11*(3), 108-117.

Li, Q., & Li, Y. (2018). An empirical study on the proactive role of internal audit in enterprise risk management. *Journal of Finance and Accounting Research, 6*(4), 216-222.

Li, X., & Li, J. (2019). Integration of internal audit with risk management in Chinese companies. *Journal of Accounting in Emerging Economies, 9*(3), 341-357.

Li, X., & Li, Y. (2020). The roles of internal auditors in China: A balancing act between auditing and advising. *Accounting Research, 7*(3), 79-89.

Li, Z., & Li, Y. (2020). Balancing the roles of internal auditors in China: Insights from a survey of chief audit executives. *Managerial Auditing Journal, 35*(1), 40-62.

Liu, L., Li, M., & Yang, J. (2021). Internal audit quality, financial performance, and corporate social responsibility: Evidence from China. *The British Accounting Review, 53*(1), 100945.

Liu, Q., Zhang, Y., Wang, J., & Huang, Z. (2018). Research on the integration of internal audit and risk management. *Journal of Finance and Economics, 44*(11), 129-137.

Liu, Y., Chen, L., & Wang, Q. (2018). Internal audit and risk management integration: Evidence from China. *Journal of Financial Crime, 25*(1), 80-93.

Liu, Y., Wang, Q., & Chen, L. (2019). The talent shortage of internal audit in China: A survey of the market. *Managerial Auditing Journal, 34*(2), 164-179.

Liu, Y., Wang, X., Wu, J., & Li, H. (2019). Research on the development of internal audit in China. *Accounting Research, 6,* 63-68.

McCombes, S. (2022, November 30). *Survey research | Definition, examples & methods.* Scribbr. https://www.scribbr.com/methodology/survey-research/

McCombes, S. (2022, October 10). *Descriptive research | Definition, types, methods & examples.* Scribbr. https://www.scribbr.com/methodology/descriptive-research/

McDonald Consulting Group. (2023). *How many internal auditors should you train.* https://mcdcg.com/training/many-internal-auditors-train/#:~:text=The%20ideal%20guideline%2C%20for%20your,of%20employees%20within%20the%20organization.

Muruganandham, R., Venkatesh, K., Devadasan, S. R., & Harish, V. (2023). TQM through the integration of blockchain with ISO 9001:2015 standard based quality management system. *Total Quality Management & Business Excellence 34*(3-4), 291-311. https://doi.org/10.1080/14783363.2021.1911635

Nabulsi, H., & Haidoura, H. M. (2018). Making a difference through internal audit leadership and enterprise risk management. *IOSR Journal of Economics and Finance (IOSR-JEF), 9*(2), 52-60. https://www.iosrjournals.org/iosr-jef/papers/Vol9-Issue2/Version-1/H0902015260.pdf

Nikolopoulou, K. (2022, December 1). *What is purposive sampling? | Definition & examples.* Scribbr. https://www.scribbr.com/methodology/purposive-sampling/

Olavsrud, T. (2016, March 09). *5 characteristics of exceptional internal audit leaders.* CIO. https://www.cio.com/article/240475/5-characteristics-of-exceptional-internal-audit-leaders.html

Paranoan, N., Roreng, P. P., Tandirerung, C. J., & Tandungan, E. S. (2018). Disclosing professionalism behaviour of internal auditor in preventing fraud by using the local cultural wisdom 'Longko' (A case study at

Toraja tribe, south Sulawesi, Indonesia). *KnE Social Sciences.* https://doi.org/10.18502/kss.v3i10.3462

Praise, I., & Rapina, R. (2022). The role of internal audit, leadership effectiveness, and organizational culture in risk management effectiveness. *European Journal of Management Issues, 30*(2), 83-91. https://doi.org/10.15421/192208

PwC. (2021). COVID-19: Impacts on Internal Audit. https://www.pwc.com/us/en/library/covid-19/covid-19-impacts-on-internal-audit.html

Scherer, T. (2020, July 14*). 6 benefits of internal auditing.* Reciprocity. https://reciprocity.com/6-benefits-of-internal-auditing/

Sukirman, Hidayah, R., Suryandari, R., Kayati, I. N., Rahayuningsih, B., Aini, S., Riski, N., & Muslikhin. (2021). Environmental control, internal auditor, and good university governance. *E3S Web of Conferences, 317,* 05016. https://doi.org/10.1051/e3sconf /202131705016

The Institute of Internal Auditors. (2017). *International professional practices framework (IPPF).* Altamonte Springs: The Institute of Internal Auditors Research Foundation.

The Institute of Internal Auditors. (2021). *Internal audit assessment tool for audit committees.* https://www.theiia.org/globalassets/documents/communications/2021/january/internal-audit-assessment-tool.pdf

The Institute of Internal Auditors. (2022). *Internal audit competency framework.* IIA. https://www.theiia.org/globalassets/documents/standards/ia-competency-framework/2022-4103-sem-competency-framework-graphics-table_fnl.pdf

Tuanakotta, T. M. (2016). *Mendeteksi manipulasi laporan keuangan.* Salemba Empat.

Wang, Y., & Sun, X. (2021). Internal audit in China: An Overview and Future Directions. *Accounting Horizons, 35*(1), 127-141.

Wang, Y., & Wu, X. (2020). Research on the improvement of internal audit management in the construction industry in China. *Journal of Business and Management, 8*(1), 23-28

Wang, Z., Wen, J., Wu, X., & Chen, S. (2020). Enhancing internal auditing in China: Insights from a survey of internal auditors. *Journal of Business Research, 119,* 254-264.

Whitehouse, T. (2016, April 19). *To be a great internal auditor, be a great communicator.* Compliance Week. https://www.complianceweek.com/to-be-a-great-internal-auditor-be-a-great-communicator/3055.article

Wu, H., Liu, Y., & Yan, J. (2019). Regulatory requirements and internal audit in China: An empirical study. *Journal of Financial Regulation and Compliance, 27*(3), 331-348.

Wu, Z., Li, X., & Li, Y. (2019). Study on the regulatory requirements of internal audit management in China. *Journal of Audit and Economics, 5,* 74-78.

Zhang, L., & Zhang, H. (2019). The adoption of international standards in internal audit in China: A literature review. *Journal of Modern Accounting and Auditing, 15*(8), 403-411.

Zhang, Y., & Xu, Y. (2019). The analysis of the internal audit management of construction enterprises in China. *Journal of Engineering,* 1-6.

Zhao, J., & Li, Z. (2019). Research on the current situation and countermeasures of internal audit management in China's construction enterprises. *Journal of Business and Economic Development, 8*(1), 25-30.

Zhao, J., & Li, Z. (2019). Research on the current situation and countermeasures of internal audit management in China's construction enterprises. *Journal of Business and Economic Development, 8*(1), 25-30.

Zhou, X. (2020). Research on the internal audit management of construction enterprises in China. Advances in Social Science, *Education and Humanities Research, 548,* 573-576.